THE PRACTICAL GUIDE TO
KEELBOAT
SAILING

THE PRACTICAL GUIDE TO
KEELBOAT
SAILING

LEARN ALL THE ESSENTIAL SKILLS WITH OVER 300 STEP-BY-STEP EXPERT PHOTOGRAPHS AND DIAGRAMS

JEREMY EVANS

LORENZ BOOKS

This edition is published by Lorenz Books, an imprint of Anness Publishing Ltd, Hermes House,
88–89 Blackfriars Road, London SE1 8HA; tel. 020 7401 2077; fax 020 7633 9499

www.lorenzbooks.com; www.annesspublishing.com

If you like the images in this book and would like to investigate using them for
publishing, promotions or advertising, please visit our website
www.practicalpictures.com for more information.

UK agent: The Manning Partnership Ltd;
tel. 01225 478444; fax 01225 478440; sales@manning-partnership.co.uk
UK distributor: Grantham Book Services Ltd;
tel. 01476 541080; fax 01476 541061; orders@gbs.tbs-ltd.co.uk
North American agent/distributor: National Book Network;
tel. 301 459 3366; fax 301 429 5746; www.nbnbooks.com
Australian agent/distributor: Pan Macmillan Australia;
tel. 1300 135 113; fax 1300 135 103; customer.service@macmillan.com.au
New Zealand agent/distributor: David Bateman Ltd;
tel. (09) 415 7664; fax (09) 415 8892

Publisher: JOANNA LORENZ
Editorial Director: JUDITH SIMONS
Project Editor: FELICITY FORSTER
Designer: GOWERS ELMES LTD
Photography: OCEAN IMAGES
Illustrations: CREATIVE BYTE
Production Controller: CLAIRE RAE

ETHICAL TRADING POLICY

Because of our ongoing ecological investment programme, you, as our customer, can have the
pleasure and reassurance of knowing that a tree is being cultivated on your behalf to naturally
replace the materials used to make the book you are holding. For further information about
this scheme, go to www.annesspublishing.com/trees

Previously published as *Keelboat Sailing*

Although some of the photographs in this book show people sailing without a lifevest or
buoyancy aid, the author and publisher wish to stress that they strongly advise their use
for all sailing situations. In most cases there are no laws or regulations regarding the use
of lifevests, although they are invariably mandatory at sailing schools. Sailing is above
all about taking responsibility for your own decisions and actions.

Contents

Introduction

Yacht sailing began as a sport for wealthy gentlemen in the 19th century, at a time when steam and diesel were in the process of making sails redundant for commercial and naval use. A historic race was staged around the Isle of Wight off the south coast of England on 22nd August 1851, with The Royal Yacht Squadron's Hundred Pound Cup made by Garrard of London as

BELOW **A modern America's Cup racer sails out with a late 19th-century J-Class yacht. Both were specifically designed to race for the same trophy, although in different eras.**

the prize. Its name was changed to the America's Cup in honour of the winning schooner *America*, and this was the start of modern yacht racing as we know it today.

Since those early beginnings the rich have continued to enjoy the sport of keelboat racing at high profile events such as Antigua Race Week, the Aga Khan Cup at Porto Cervo and the La Nioulargue regatta for vintage racing yachts at St Tropez. However, yacht racing has grown into a popular world-wide sport that is certainly not only

the preserve of the rich and famous, with events such as the Round the Isle Race (round the Isle of Wight, like that early race) attracting a huge entry with thousands of people enjoying the event each year. Open keelboat racing is long established as an Olympic sport – currently for the Soling and Yngling classes – while a host of other traditional and modern designs ranging from Sunbeams to Etchells provide intense competition for two or three crew at local and national regattas. Sportsboats such as the Beneteau

25, Melges 24 and the Hunter 707 are day-racing keelboats that provide dinghy-style excitement and performance, and demand a high level of expertise from the crew.

At the other end of the spectrum, cruising in a keelboat with proper accommodation is a wonderful way to escape from the stresses of everyday life, and a massive choice of yachts at all sizes and prices has made the sport available for all. You don't even need to own a boat to experience sailing. If you like the idea of racing, willing crews are in demand at every level, and time rather than money is the commitment that is required to enjoy the sport. If you prefer to indulge in the relaxed cruising of family sailing, there are many options available. You can charter a yacht for a week or two in the Caribbean or Mediterranean for a spell of sailing in the sun, join a yacht flotilla, which will ensure that expert help is always on hand, sign up for a full course of tuition at a cruising school or simply enjoy a trip on a yacht owned by friends.

Sailing has so much to offer. There's the sheer exhilaration of experiencing two elements – wind and water – and learning to contain

ABOVE **All you want is fine weather, a calm anchorage in a beautiful setting and a comfortable yacht to live on. That's not much to ask for! This charter yacht is in the Turkish Aegean.**

BELOW **First launched in 1996, the Melges 24 is considered the most successful sportsboat in the world. It is raced and sailed internationally and provides the very top levels of competition.**

and control them. But keelboat sailing is much more than that. You can sail to new places close to home, or perhaps realize a dream of sailing round the world. The basic skills are not difficult to acquire and can soon provide enough expertise to give endless fun and pleasure, but beyond that there is a lifetime of experience waiting for you – just turn the pages to appreciate what lies ahead...

Sailing
Basics

All sailing techniques start from a set of basic principles that govern the skills required to utilize whatever wind is available. At their most basic, the skills of sailing towards the wind and away from the wind are very simple, but that surmise requires perfect conditions meaning flat water, a steady breeze and no obstacles. Real sailing is seldom like that, with the wind yo-yoing up and down, waves forming, tides running and other boats getting in the way. Nor are sailing boats so simple that you just steer and pull pieces of string. Handling a yacht requires many other skills such as modern navigation, VHF radio communication, interpreting the weather, rights of way, manoeuvring under power, anchoring or mooring, looking after the needs of the crew, ensuring all safety practices are followed, and managing and maintaining everything on board.

The moral is that keelboat sailing technique is an exceptionally wide-ranging subject that can be learnt at all manner of levels. It can also be learnt quickly, but there is nothing like practice combined with experience to ensure that the lessons are learnt well.

How a sailboat moves

At its simplest, wind pushes a sail from behind, which is known as running downwind. Sailing a few degrees either side of downwind was the only direction in which the old-fashioned square-riggers could go, and if the wind was blowing in the wrong direction they would simply have to wait days or weeks for it to change. Thankfully the modern style of Bermudan rig came along to change all that, and now sailboats can sail in almost any direction with the obvious exception of straight into the wind; the more sophisticated and performance-oriented the sailboat, the closer to the wind it will be able to go.

The ability to sail towards the wind rather than just away from it is achieved by the aerofoil effect of modern sails. Wind flowing over the sails is composed of a moving mass of air particles that separates when it hits the front or leading edge of the sail. From there it accelerates around both sides, following the curved shape of the sail to produce positive high pressure on the windward side (the side the wind is blowing on to) and negative low pressure on the leeward side (the side the wind is

ABOVE **With sails pulled hard in, a keelboat can sail towards the direction the wind is coming from. The sails and keel provide lift to windward on this Swallow, a design from 1946.**

blowing away from). The difference between this positive and negative pressure creates the aerodynamic force that sucks the sail forwards and drives the boat along, generating sufficient force to overcome the natural resistance of water

against the lower part of the hull as well as air resistance against the top of the hull, sails, rigging, fittings and crew.

Sail camber and incidence

The cross-sectional shape of a sail will help determine its performance. The degree of curvature (camber) must be correctly aligned with the apparent wind (the angle of incidence) to produce maximum drive. The optimum angle of incidence is widely held to be at 15 degrees between the chord (an imaginary straight line connecting both ends of the sail) and the apparent wind. If the angle of incidence is greater, airflow will detach from the leeward side creating turbulence and reducing drive. If the angle of incidence is smaller, the sail will stall as positive air flow ceases to flow over the windward side.

The amount of camber and its position in the sail will greatly effect performance characteristics. All modern

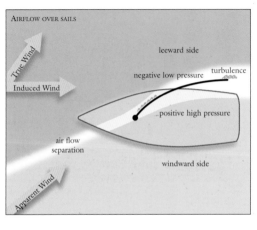

AIRFLOW OVER SAILS

True Wind

Induced Wind

leeward side

negative low pressure   turbulence

Apparent Wind

air flow separation

positive high pressure

windward side

LEFT **Airflow over sails separates on to the windward (high pressure) and leeward (low pressure) sides, and turbulence is created at the leading and trailing edges. The sails must always be adjusted to make maximum use of the speed and direction of the apparent wind.**

high performance keelboats provide adjustment systems to alter luff (leading edge) and foot tension, which will maximize or minimize camber as well as changing the position of maximum camber fore and aft from the midpoint of the sail.

True wind and apparent wind

The wind's force in a sail is concentrated in an area known as the centre of effort (CE) while the outer area of the sail plays a secondary role in keeping the power of the wind under control. This concept can be directly experienced by windsurfers who hold up the rig and can effectively feel the centre of effort pulling between their hands.

Windsurfers also have the most direct experience of the difference between true wind and apparent wind, a concept that is important with keelboat sailing. **True wind** is the real wind. In terms of speed and direction it is the wind experienced by a stationary observer. **Apparent wind** is the wind experienced by any moving object. For instance, if a cyclist is cycling at 16kph (10mph) directly into an oncoming wind, which has a true speed of 16kph (10mph), the apparent wind he or she has to contend with will total 32kph (20mph). Conversely, if the cyclist is cycling in exactly the same direction as the wind, and both are moving at 16kph (10mph), the apparent wind will be zero. The speed of true wind and apparent wind will never be the same when a boat is moving. Apparent wind is at its lightest when a boat is travelling in the same direction (running dead downwind) as true wind, and becomes progressively stronger as a boat sails closer to the wind. This phenomenon also has a marked effect on the difference in temperature when sailing downwind and upwind.

The direction of true and apparent wind will only be the same when a boat is travelling in the same direction (running dead downwind). On any other course the

RIGHT **As a boat accelerates, the direction of the apparent wind changes and comes from further ahead. This is particularly noticeable on a fast cruiser like this trimaran.**

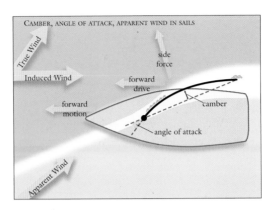

CAMBER, ANGLE OF ATTACK, APPARENT WIND IN SAILS

True Wind

Induced Wind

side force

forward drive

forward motion

camber

Apparent Wind

angle of attack

LEFT **The main sheet or jib sheet is the primary control used to control the angle of incidence or angle of attack. This is done by adjusting the position of the sail relative to airflow. Adjusting the sail at the deepest point or camber is equivalent to tuning the sail to maximize performance.**

apparent wind will come from further forward (the direction the boat is heading towards) than the true wind. This is the induced direction of the wind as a result of the boat's forward progress. The greater the speed of the boat, the more the direction of the wind will move forward, which is why the fastest sail-powered craft for their size – windsurfers and catamarans – must always have their sails pulled hard in when they are sailing at speed in order to maximize the apparent wind.

Slipping sideways (leeway)

Because of their design, sails cannot achieve a pure forward force. Instead, most of the force is sideways, and becomes progressively more as a boat sails closer to the wind.

The sideways force must be converted into forward speed instead of driving the boat sideways or blowing it on to its side. On dinghies this is largely achieved by the use of a centreboard or daggerboard to provide leeward resistance, combined with minimizing hull and air resistance to allow the boat to move forwards and the crew's skills to keep the boat upright.

Fixed keels

A ballasted keel provides the same solution for resting sideways force, and the closer the design is to a long, deep daggerboard the more efficient it will be. However, a fixed keel is less practical for cruising as the yacht can only moor in deep water, and is very sensitive to gusts.

Hull and air resistance

These are related to the speed and course of a boat, the wind speed and direction, and water conditions. Resistance due to friction under the boat is known as skin friction, and is created by individual layers of water passing beneath the boat. The solution is to reduce the amount of boat in contact with the water (wetted surface area) to a minimum, which is first achieved by design and second by the crew trimming the boat correctly.

Resistance due to the shape of the hull (form resistance) is mainly caused by hitting waves, plus the turbulence created by the imperfect shapes of bows, stern, rudder, keel, propeller and other appendages. Form resistance decreases in proportion to the weight of the boat, and is the factor that prevents displacement boats such as keelboats from accelerating. They create a single wave, from bow to stern, from which they cannot escape.

Means of reducing form resistance include: producing a boat to minimum weight at the design stage, sailing with

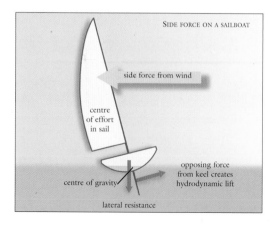

SIDE FORCE ON A SAILBOAT

side force from wind

centre of effort in sail

centre of gravity

opposing force from keel creates hydrodynamic lift

lateral resistance

LEFT The side forces on a sailboat act on the rig, sails and hull, which are pushed one way, while the keel provides a counter balance. It helps to transform the sideways movement into forward movement, as well as providing resistance against the sailboat heeling.

minimum weight, trimming the boat correctly both fore and aft and sideways, and ensuring the stern does not drag and create turbulence, which may also be created by an incorrectly profiled rudder.

Resistance due to heeling of the boat increases in form resistance in direct relation to the angle of heel and so most yachts should be sailed as upright as the given conditions will possibly allow.

RIGHT The density and position of the ballast will determine how a yacht performs. At the extremes of high performance, weight is concentrated at the bottom of the keel.

Resistance due to leeway (induced drag) builds up turbulence on the leeward side of the boat as form resistance increases. This can be cured by sailing the boat as flat as possible and driving the boat forwards, which is a specific skill.

Wind resistance on hull, rigging and anything else that stands out is most apparent when sailing close to the wind. The solution is to make the outline of a boat as clean as possible, using internal halyards, which do not break up airflow round the sail, combined with minimalist rigging and no unnecessary protuberances. Wind resistance caused by the physical bulk of the crew is likely to be minimal, and it is more important for the crew to sit in the right place to trim the boat correctly.

Resistance caused by sailing through rough water is best solved by technique to keep the boat driving and prevent it stalling on waves.

Keeping upright

All sailboats are designed to be sailed virtually upright, particularly dinghies that have nearly flat bottoms, to maximize their planing ability and ensure that the boat is sailed efficiently and that it is moving quickly over the water.

Yachts have a fixed keel weighted (ballasted) with lead. The centre of gravity – which depends on how much weight is in the keel – is lower than the centre of buoyancy, which is within the yacht.

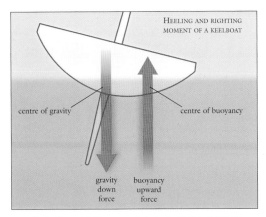

HEELING AND RIGHTING
MOMENT OF A KEELBOAT

centre of gravity

centre of buoyancy

gravity
down
force

buoyancy
upward
force

ABOVE **The heeling and righting moment of a keelboat will depend on the position of the centre of gravity. This is much lower than in a dinghy and will depend on the length and relative weight of the fully ballasted keel.**

ABOVE **Getting all the crew to sit up on the windward (weather) deck of a yacht will help keep it upright, but the effect is slight when compared to a crew hiking out on a dinghy. Sitting outside the guardrails is not allowed.**

The behaviour of a keelboat is different since its centre of gravity, principally the weight of the yacht itself – is much lower down and will remain lower than the centre of buoyancy which is within the yacht. The righting arm between the centre of gravity and centre of buoyancy actually gets longer as the angle of heel increases, which means that the yacht's resistance to heeling increases. So while a yacht may be blown almost flat, there will be minimal heeling moment induced by the sails, and the ballasted keel will soon bring her back upright, albeit with her bow slewing into the wind. There are exceptions. If a yacht is held down by an out of control spinnaker or knocked down by waves, its cockpit could fill with water. This has caused a few sinkings, but it is a rare occurrence limited mainly to small, open keelboats racing on inshore waters or yachts caught in extreme conditions. These can occur in confused waters on a coastal shelf after a storm, as in the open wilds of the southern oceans where well publicized capsizes have been the result of racing yachts losing their keel.

LEFT **In normal conditions a yacht will not capsize, since the righting arm between the centre of buoyancy and centre of gravity gets longer as the yacht heels further, while the effect of wind on the sails is reduced. This means that a yacht can only be capsized by a wave, or an accumulation of waves, in very extreme weather conditions.**

Where and when to sail

Sailing probably qualifies as a risk sport, although the risks are so minimal for those who take care that fatalities or serious injuries are extremely rare. However, one should always have great respect for the elements of wind and water, particularly when sailing near a coast.

Safe locations

When starting out, the ultimate safe sailing location would probably be a fresh water lake or reservoir of no more than 1.6km (1 mile) diameter, with an even depth, warm water, a regular, steady wind of Force 4 maximum, a club to sail from and non-stop rescue cover.

Lee shores

A lee shore (a shoreline that the wind is blowing on to) was a terrifying prospect for all the old square-rigged ships. It was

a lee shore in Ireland that became the wrecking ground for the Spanish Armada. Their captains often found themselves in an impossible position, blown on to inhospitable lee shores with no ability to sail upwind and escape the danger. To this day a lee shore in strong winds can still be extremely dangerous for modern yachts sailing offshore, as was demonstrated by the loss of the famous racing yacht *Morning Cloud* (owned by the former British Prime Minister, Edward Heath) together with two of her crew off the south coast of England in 1974.

Crowded water and shores

It is a fact of modern life that all popular pastimes attract crowds, and sailing is no exception to the rule. Always be aware of beach users and swimmers when launching and landing. In an ideal

situation swimmers and boats should be separated by lanes, but there are times when swimmers will still cross your path.

Be thoughtful and considerate towards other boat users. When launching or mooring wait your turn; leave plenty of space for other boats to manoeuvre; help others and they will help you. Beware of boats that are anchored or moored close by. Give them a wide berth and if in doubt always aim to pass downwind (or down tide if applicable) of them.

Beware of powercrafts. Power gives way to sail, but some powerboat owners are unaware or oblivious to this, go much too fast, and often have very little comprehension of the problems of manoeuvring a small sailboat. Jet-skis have a particularly bad reputation, but large powercrafts can be equally lethal.

LEFT **One of the prime rules of sailing is "Keep a good lookout." This Flying 15 keelboat has windows in the jib and mainsail.**

ABOVE **Yachting is popular and summer berths can get very congested! Always be considerate to your neighbours.**

WATCHING THE WEATHER

Dressing correctly for the conditions, in particular wearing efficient waterproofs with thermal underwear and protecting your head from heat loss, is essential when sailing in very cold weather. The good news is that excellent clothing is available.

Sailing in cold water

Exposure to water temperatures below 20°C (68°F) needs to be treated with progressive seriousness as the temperature decreases and the time increases. Very cold water below 10°C (50°F) may be experienced when sailing on freshwater lakes and reservoirs, where temperatures are potentially at their lowest in spring. This is just when many people start to sail after winter, and a sunny spring sky is all that is necessary to lull them into a false sense of security.

Hypothermia

Prolonged exposure to cold water causes hypothermia (acute heat loss) and is eventually fatal. The timescale is very short. Tests have shown that an average person in normal clothes loses consciousness after 20 minutes of floating in water of 10°C (50°F), and death usually follows. If they attempt to splash around to keep warm, the heat loss will be even faster.

ABOVE **If you fall off the boat, cold water can kill. It is a wise precaution for all crew to wear lifejackets in the cockpit and clip on harness lines if moving forward.**

Before losing consciousness there are two phases. During the first phase, the person in the water is alert and has the will and ability to participate in his or her rescue; during the second phase, the person's will to survive is effectively lost and rescue becomes totally dependent on outside assistance.

ABOVE **It may be sunny but it can be bitterly cold. Advances in clothing design have made a tremendous difference to sailing enjoyment and turned it into an effective all-seasons sport.**

Treating hypothermia

First stage Shivering, looking cold, complaining of cold. Time to head for the shore without delay.
Second stage Lethargy, drowsiness or confusion followed by numbness, cramp, nausea, slurred speech and eventual loss of consciousness.
Action If a person complains of the cold or shows any symptoms of moving towards the second stage of hypothermia, keep them warm and get them ashore as soon as possible. Get them out of the wind and provide them with dry clothing/coverings. If their condition deteriorates or fails to improve, seek urgent medical attention.

ABOVE **Offshore sailors know they have to dress correctly to enjoy whistling along at high speeds in all weathers. The faster the boat, the more you need to dress up. Apparent wind from ahead (wind speed plus boat speed) will always be colder than apparent wind from behind (wind speed less boat speed).**

ABOVE **Children can suffer badly from the cold while sailing. Dress them up, keep them busy and put them in charge of the boat.**

Wind chill

It's always warmer out of the wind, and the stronger the apparent wind on a boat the more it will chill the crew. This is why catamaran sailors always need to dress for colder sailing conditions than those who sail at slow speeds. As an example, an air temperature of 20°C (68°F), rated as warm in zero wind, will become progressively cooler as the wind passes a Force 2 breeze (4–6 knots) and be rated cold at a Force 6 (22–27 knots). By comparison a very cold air temperature of 5°C (41°F) will become icy cold at Force 6 (22–27 knots).

Wind chill is dependent on what you are wearing, how much of your body is exposed, whether you are wet and your general fitness and body temperature.

Wind chill is not so important in air temperatures of 30°C (86°F) and beyond when a warm wind is guaranteed, but beware the possibility of a thunderstorm or heavy rainfall, which can make the temperature drop dramatically.

RIGHT **When sailing in hot weather, the effects of wind chill may become irrelevant due to the warmth of the wind, so that sunburn combined with dehydration becomes a more pressing problem. However, if a thunderstorm occurs the temperature will lower dramatically, and hypothermia becomes a real possibility.**

ABOVE **Good-quality sunglasses are vital for sailing in strong sunlight, both to protect your eyes and see where you are going. Wear them with prescription lenses if required.**

ABOVE **The reflection of water combined with the white hull and super-structure of a dinghy or yacht provides a medium in which the effects of the hot sun are magnified. Stripping your shirt off could be hazardous.**

Beware the sun

Sailors in cold climates can seldom get enough of it, but when sailing in hot temperatures the sun needs to be treated with caution. The effect of a cooling wind can be very misleading and, when combined with the effect of strong sun reflected off the water, can lead to severe sunburn, which is exacerbated by the drying effect of a salty sea. Sailors are always advised to use sun block (SPF 15 or higher) on exposed body parts in strong sunlight, and if they burn easily to ensure that their body is suitably covered with lightweight protection and to wear a hat.

A secondary effect of strong sun is dehydration. It is easy to ignore or even not to notice the effects of drying out while sailing, until symptoms, which include a parched mouth and a muzzy, tired, headachy feeling, become apparent. The best cure is prevention, making sure

to drink enough liquid throughout the day to ward off the onset of dehydration. Plain water is as good as anything and on most keelboats you can store it quite easily in large plastic bottles.

If dehydration does begin to get to you, the first thing to do is to seek protection from the sun. Head for the shore and shade, or take refuge behind or even under a lowered sail.

LEFT **The proliferation of skin cancer has struck a chord in countries such as Australia where the sun ethic is being tempered by the need to avoid full exposure.**

Lost in the fog?

A sea fog or sea fret is a common phenomenon in early summer at the start and end of the day. It relies on the heat of the land to burn off as the morning progresses, but frustratingly fog may linger on the coastal stretch where the warm land meets the cold sea. Fog should be avoided at all costs for the following reasons:

• There will be zero or very little wind at all.
• It will be cold, clammy and unpleasant.
• Getting lost in fog is very easy and the chances of collision are high. Be wary of sound signals such as hooters and horns, it can be difficult to tell where they are coming from.
• You need to keep well clear of shipping lanes and out of the way of powercrafts who are relying on radar unable to detect a small boat and that are travelling too fast.
• Persistent fog has a habit of clearing, and then rolling back in to envelop the sea. It is better to wait until all fog has cleared before launching.

ABOVE **Murky conditions can deteriorate and if fog drops down it becomes an unnerving experience. Careful navigation using radar and GPS plays a vital role in ensuring the crew's safety. Here the navigator is using traditional chart work on the 70-foot training yacht John Laing.**

Thunderstorms and lightning

The problem with thunderstorms is that they are often unexpected. Following a period of humidity and light winds, there will be a sudden drop in temperature accompanied by fierce gusts of wind fanning out from the leading edges of the storm. Sailors can easily be caught off guard by the heavy rain, cold air and the violence of the wind, and if you are unprepared in terms of technique or clothing, capsize and hypothermia become real possibilities. It is rare for yachts to be struck by lightning, particularly when out on the water. All you can do is be philosophical; lightning must strike somewhere, but the chances of being injured or killed by lightning while sailing are remote.

Most thunderstorms are created inland when the ground becomes overheated. A thermal low leads to falling pressure over the land and rising pressure out to sea, and as the unstable air from the thermal low shoots high into the sky it forms massive cumulonimbus clouds along with thunder and lightning.

If the thunderstorm is moving offshore against an onshore wind, it will suck up this wind and throw back a downdraught gale, creating violent gusts, which are often followed by heavy rain or hailstones. The effects can be most extreme on inland lakes surrounded by high mountains, with downdraughts of Force 6 (27 knots) or more tearing into the surface of the lake and kicking up a violent sea. Some lakes in Italy and Switzerland are so prone to this phenomenon that storm warning lights and flags are on regular stand-by.

The most obvious sign of an impending thunderstorm is a heavy and oppressive feeling in the air, while on land everything, in particular the birds,

LEFT **Inland lakes surrounded by high mountains – such as Lake Geneva – can be prone to violent thunderstorms in warm weather. Be prepared for high winds, and make sure you have sufficient clothing to cope with a considerable drop in temperature. These multihulls are racing in the annual Bol d'Or long-distance race.**

LEFT **A beautiful hot-weather sailing location such as the Mediterranean can also be a breeding ground for dangerous thunderstorms. Conditions can change quickly, so listen to the forecasts, watch the sky and always be prepared to up anchor and move on.**

appears to go silent. The first rolls of thunder can be heard up to about 16km (10 miles) away and, if the thunder is clearly coming your way, you can reckon that the usual rate of progress is about 19kph (12mph). This allows only a modest time to prepare yourself by putting on waterproof and windproof clothing, or to seek shelter on land. Needless to say it is prudent to avoid standing alone on the shoreline, and keep well away from solitary trees.

UNDERSTANDING WINDS

Without winds you cannot sail, but it is exceptionally rare to have no wind at all. This is when you are totally becalmed, a state which seldom lasts for more than a few hours as eventually the wind will fill in from some direction.

Wind direction

The direction and speed of the wind will be graphically displayed on all visual weather forecasts. The wind blows along the

isobars, keeping low pressure to the left and high pressure to the right. However, the isobars show the wind direction at about 600m (2,000ft), and the surface wind over the coastline will back (move anti-clockwise) about 15 degrees from the isobar direction due to friction on the earth's surface. The most reliable way to check wind direction and speed before you launch is to consult an anemometer (wind speed indicator). Less precise methods include looking at flags or smoke, watching boats out on the water, and listening to the wind at different angles – it sounds loudest when you face directly into the wind.

The ideal wind direction for launching is sideshore, when the wind is blowing parallel to the shoreline. This should allow you to sail out on a reaching course, turn

RIGHT **All sailors love a fresh wind that provides a fast and exhilarating ride! In typical summer conditions the seabreeze kicks in during the afternoon and may increase to Force 4 or more.**

LEFT A typical summer pattern is for the onshore seabreeze to die in the early evening and be replaced by a light offshore wind during the night which may linger in the early morning. The wind will then change direction to a seabreeze, building through the afternoon.

round, and sail back in on the opposite reach, before turning parallel to the beach to come head to wind and slow the boat to a stop before landing. The more onshore (blowing on to the shore) the direction of the wind is, the more problems you are likely to have. A side-onshore wind of Force 2+ (4–6 knots) may start stacking up waves, but should still allow you to sail straight out from the beach. A dead-onshore wind will push in waves that drive the boat back, and mean that you have to sail out at an angle across the waves. Offshore winds, blowing away from the shore, should be treated with particular caution. An offshore wind, which appears zephyr-like close in by the beach, will gain strength as you move away from the shore. This effect can be extreme if you sail off a shoreline protected by high ground. The light, gusty wind will soon pick up and, if you can't handle the conditions and start to capsize, your boat will be driven further offshore where the wind gets progressively stronger and your difficulties increase.

Lulls and gusts

These are caused by rising and sinking air on days when cumulus clouds indicate an unstable wind pattern. Because the gusts come straight from above they will veer (turn clockwise) in a direction more closely aligned with the isobars. The gust may last for a few minutes, followed by a lull when the wind backs to its original direction. The difference in the wind shift direction is an important tactical consideration in all yacht racing.

Wind speed

On a weather map closely spaced isobars generally indicate strong winds, while wide spacing means light winds. If the gap between the isobars halves, the wind speed doubles.

LEFT Yachts can be equipped with all kinds of electronic aids that measure wind speed and direction, but it is still good to "feel the wind on your ears". This style of sailing suits fast, lightweight boats such as trimarans.

LEFT Wind shifts play a major role in deciding tactical success in racing. They become particularly important in a one-design class where boats can be tacked with minimal loss of speed. The two X One Design open keelboats shown racing here are a class that was originally designed in 1909, but is still going strong with some help from modern materials. They are only allowed to be raced with wooden hulls and spars, but the plan for the rig has been updated. Around 170 X One Design boats are in everyday use, with fleets at Cowes, Poole and Chichester Harbour in southern England. They carry a small spinnaker and are normally raced with three crew.

The perfect sailing breeze will depend on ability. Beginners will prefer a light wind, but not so light that it is difficult to assess where the wind is blowing from or keep the boat moving. For most beginners winds between Force 1 and 3 (1–10 knots) should be suitable. Those with more experience will enjoy sailing in stronger winds. Force 3–4 (7–16 knots) represents perfect sailing conditions. Force 5–6 (17–27 knots) becomes considerably more demanding, but should be viewed in the context of the sailing location. Low air temperatures, cold water and the effect of tides and waves are likely to make such winds considerably more challenging than when sailing close to the shore in a warm, tideless location.

Despite Force 6 (22–27 knots) being described by Admiral Beaufort as merely a strong breeze it is in effect very windy. Beyond Force 6 conditions become extremely unpleasant.

Summer winds

Seabreezes are created by the sun warming up the land ahead of the comparatively cold sea, and are mainly a coastal, summer phenomenon that will continue to blow no more than 48km (30 miles) inland. They are most effective when the change from cold night to hot day is reliable and pronounced, but will not work if the land is shrouded by cloud. A typical seabreeze location is the eastern Mediterranean where the afternoon summer wind turns on like clockwork on most days.

A regular coastal pattern is for the seabreeze to gradually cancel out the effect of any night wind that has been blowing offshore. A period of calm and irregular wind ensues, before the seabreeze is established in the early afternoon and provides a steady onshore wind of Force 4 (11–16 knots); perfect for summer sailing.

The seabreeze will then die away to a calm as the land starts to cool in the early evening.

Lakes that are surrounded by mountains can also be affected by summer winds. A well-known example is Lake Garda in northern Italy. There, the light wind that generally blows from the mountains during the night and early morning is replaced by a stronger valley wind in the opposite direction towards the sunny side of the mountains. The result is a strong, predictable wind on summer afternoons.

ABOVE Piles of cumulus clouds indicate a weather pattern with frequent gusts and lulls creating wind shifts. The timing of the gusts can be critical when racing.

Admiral Beaufort's scale of wind force

Distances over the sea are measured in nautical miles (1 nautical mile equals 1,853.27 metres, 2,025 yards or 1.15 statute miles), and wind speed is measured in nautical miles per hour or knots. These knots are divided into wind forces, which describe the speed of the wind. This system, invented by Admiral Beaufort in the 18th century, is still in use today with modern updates, describing likely conditions both inland and on the open ocean. Conditions on protected coastal waters will generally be less marked, but in some instances may be more extreme if there is a tidal influence.

Force	Description	Velocity
0	Calm	Less than 1 knot (less than 1kph)
	Smoke rises vertically.	
	Sea like a mirror.	
1	Light air	1–3 knots (1–5kph/1–3mph)
	Direction of wind shown by smoke drift, but not by wind vanes.	
	Ripples like fish scales form on the sea.	
2	Light breeze	4–6 knots (6–12kph/4–7mph)
	Wind felt on face. Leaves rustle. Ordinary vane moved by wind.	
	Small wavelets, still short but more pronounced.	
3	Gentle breeze	7–10 knots (12–19kph/8–12mph)
	Leaves and small twigs in constant motion. Wind extends light flags.	
	Large wavelets. Crests beginning to break.	
4	Moderate breeze	11–16 knots (20–29kph/13–18mph)
	Raises dust and loose paper. Small branches are moved.	
	Small waves become longer. Fairly frequent white foam crests.	
5	Fresh breeze	17–21 knots (30–39kph/19–24mph)
	Small trees in leaf begin to sway. Crest wavelets form on inland waters.	
	Moderate waves taking more pronounced long form. Many white foam crests. Chance of spray.	
6	Strong breeze	22–27 knots (40–50kph/25–31mph)
	Large branches in motion. Whistling heard in telegraph wires. Umbrellas used with difficulty.	
	Large waves begin to form. White foam crests are more extensive. Probably some spray.	
7	Near gale	28–33 knots (51–61kph/32–38mph)
	Whole trees in motion. Inconvenience walking against the wind.	
	Sea heaps up and white foam from breaking waves begins to be blown in streaks along the direction of the wind.	
8	Gale	34–40 knots (62–74kph/39–46mph)
	Breaks branches off trees. Impedes progress.	
	Moderately high waves of greater length. Edges of crests begin to break into spindrift.	
9	Strong gale	41–47 knots (75–87kph/47–54mph)
	Slight structural damage such as chimney pots and slates blown away.	
	High waves. Dense streaks of foam along the direction of the wind. Crests of waves begin to topple, tumble and roll over. Spray may affect visibility.	
10	Storm	48–55 knots (88–101kph/55–63mph)
	Seldom experienced inland. Trees uprooted. Considerable structural damage occurs.	
	Very high waves with long overhanging crests. The resulting foam is blown in dense white streaks along the direction of the wind.	
11	Violent storm	56–63 knots (102–117kph/64–73mph)
	Widespread damage.	
	Exceptionally high waves sometimes concealing small and medium ships. Sea completely covered with long white patches of foam. Edges of wave crests blown into froth. Poor visibility.	
12	Hurricane	64+ knots (118kph+/73mph+)
	Widespread damage.	
	Air filled with foam and spray. Sea white with driving spray. Visibility bad.	

Waves and tides

Waves come in all types and sizes. They can either increase power on the water, or seriously tax a sailor's skills.

Ground swell waves These are generated by far off storms and can travel thousands of miles across an ocean, steadily growing in size. They approach a coastline in long, even and well-spaced parallel lines, until they hit shallow water and break. Ground swell is only experienced on open waters, and is most relevant to offshore yachts.

Wind swell waves These are wind-blown waves created by local conditions, which travel at about three-quarters of the speed of the wind. They are unlikely to get bigger than 1.5m (5ft) high, and tend to break in shallower water close to the beach. Wind swell is directly relevant to small boat sailing. The behaviour of wind swell waves will depend on the wind, tides, shoreline and other obstructions. It will also depend on the angle at which wind swell meets ground swell. If wind swell is blowing across ground swell, it can produce confused waves. If wind swell flows with or against ground swell, it can create occasional oversize waves.

Wave height The height of a wave is proportional to its length. A wave that is 7m (23ft) long can be no more than 1m (3ft) high. When it exceeds this height as it is pushed up by contact with the bottom in shallow water, it will break.

Refraction This is a phenomenon that turns waves in towards the shoreline and helps create a wave current that runs one way along the beach.

Rip A surface current where water that comes into land with the waves is allowed to flow back out to sea. It can be a fast-moving outgoing piece of water between incoming waves, and is dangerous.

Race A tidal flow around a headland that can create a dangerous maelstrom of closely spaced waves when the wind blows against the tide.

ABOVE **Wind-blown chop builds up quickly, but becomes much more challenging if the wind blows against the direction of the tide.**

ABOVE **When racing offshore the waves are likely to become much bigger, and may become confused and dangerous when wind swell and ground swell cross one another.**

Wave height international scale

The height of the face of a wave is measured by doubling the height of the back of the wave.

Code	Sea	Height
0	Calm	0m (0ft)
1	Rippled	0–0.2m (0–½ft)
2	Good	0.2–0.5m (½–1½ft)
3	Slight	0.5–1.25m (1½–4ft)
4	Moderate	1.25–2.5m (4–8ft)
5	Rough	2.5–4m (8–13ft)
6	Very rough	4–6m (13–20ft)
7	High	6–9m (20–30ft)
8	Very high	9–14m (30–46ft)
9	Huge	14m+ (46ft+)

UNDERSTANDING TIDES

With the exception of seas such as the Mediterranean, which are surrounded by land, most seas are influenced by the tide, which is directly related to the gravitational pull of the moon. The tide ebbs (flows away), turns and then floods (comes back again) in a regular cycle. How long this process takes depends on geographical location. There are three major types of tide.

Diurnal tides Mainly confined to the Tropics where they experience just one high and one low tide per lunar day. The tidal range (the difference in height between high tide and low tide) is usually small.

Semi-diurnal tides These are experienced on the Atlantic shoreline and round much of the European coast. The tide cycle takes approximately 12½ hours between successive high or low tides. For instance, if high tide (also called high water or HW) is at 6 a.m., low tide (low water or LW) will be shortly after midday with the next high tide following at 6.30 p.m. From then on the times of high or low tide will be about 50 minutes later every day.

Mixed tides Experienced along the Pacific coast of North America and on much of the Australian shoreline. These areas also

ABOVE **Be prepared! The difference between high and low tide can be extreme, with yachts left stranded and open sea replaced by a huge expanse of sand or mud at low tide.**

have two high and two low tides in a full lunar day, but there are noticeable differences in height between the first high and low and the second high and low, which becomes higher high water (HHW) and lower low water (LLW).

Tidal flow

Tides are measured in vertical height using feet or metres, and the difference between high and low tide is known as the range. The greatest range is experienced during the period known as spring tides. This is when the gravitational pull of the sun and the moon coincides, and is usually experienced around the time of a new moon and a full moon. In between this phase the range of the tide dwindles, with the smallest range experienced during a period known as neap tides, when the moon is in its first or last quarter. The timing is never precise; the spring tide with the greatest range may take place from one to three days after a new moon or a full moon. This phenomenon is also true of the neap tide, with the smallest range following the first and last quarter of the moon.

Tidal currents relate to the flow of the tide and the direction in which it is heading. The rate of flow is not consistent. As the tide approaches low or high water the current slackens before ceasing during a period known as slack water. This is when the tide turns from flood to ebb or vice versa.

ABOVE **Tidal flow will determine how far you are set off course when making a landfall. The navigator must compensate with a course that's higher or lower than the direct bearing, while also allowing for leeway.**

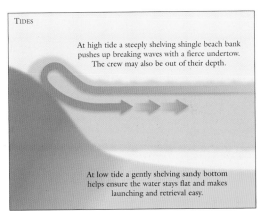

TIDES

At high tide a steeply shelving shingle beach bank pushes up breaking waves with a fierce undertow. The crew may also be out of their depth.

At low tide a gently shelving sandy bottom helps ensure the water stays flat and makes launching and retrieval easy.

ABOVE **Beware the difference between high tide and low tide. If the beach shelves steeply at high tide, it may create large crashing waves and a fierce undertow, which makes landing dangerous and may roll the boat.**

ABOVE **Knowledge of the state of the tide is vital when racing, particularly when the course is near to the shoreline where yachts will venture into shallow water to minimize the effects of tidal flow.**

The twelfths rule

To determine how far or fast the tide has risen or dropped at any given time the normal method is to use an approximate system known as the twelfths rule. The twelfths rule divides the tidal range into twelve, and in the first hour after high or low water the tide falls or rises by one-twelfth. This is the period when the tide flow is slowest. In the second hour it falls or rises a further two-twelfths. In both the third and fourth hours it falls or rises a further three-twelfths. This is the period when the tide flows fastest, beween half and three-quarter tide. In the fifth hour it falls or rises a further two-twelfths as the tidal flow begins to slow. In the final sixth hour the tide once again falls or rises by one-twelfth in the approach to slack water. This is the period when the tide flow is once again slowest.

The times and heights of tides can be found by consulting the relevant tide tables, which are widely published, sold by all good boat shops, and are on display at sailing clubs.

Tides and launching

Understanding tidal heights and times is important when launching in a tidal area. You should know in advance what happens at the opposite end of the tide. If you don't you might, for example, launch

a small trailerable keelboat at high tide, return at low tide, and discover you are miles away from the launch ramp with soggy sand in between that's impossible for your trailer to negotiate. Or you may find that the rapidly dropping tide has brought dangerous rocks, reefs and wrecks within striking distance of your keel or centreboard. Either way, the problem would be solved by understanding the tide.

You might, on the other hand, launch at low tide in a light onshore wind, then return at high tide in a much increased wind to discover that the incoming tide has advanced all the way up the gently shelving slipway where you launched and is breaking over the steeper section at the top. The sudden change in the angle of the bottom will increase the force of the waves and could make handling the boat very difficult.

ABOVE **The rise and fall of the tide means that marina pontoons will rise and fall as well. This is much easier than going alongside a wall, which requires constant adjustment of warps and springs.**

ABOVE **Low tide reveals rocks and obstructions which should be marked on the chart. As the tide rises, the reef around the rocky pillar will disappear, inviting ignorant yachtsmen to turn in too tight.**

Obstructions

Check for submerged and semi-submerged obstructions before you sail. These may range from the most obvious reefs and rocks through to wrecks, sand banks and sea defences, such as groins. Problems are most likely to occur when these obstructions cover and uncover at different states of the tide, and something that wasn't there an hour earlier suddenly meets your precious daggerboard with a sickening impact.

Tidal acceleration

The behaviour of the tide can be affected by land configuration. A narrow channel will concentrate and accelerate the tidal flow, which will be fastest in the deepest area. In extreme cases the current may flow at 10 knots or more, making it impossible to sail against the current and potentially dangerous to sail through it. A headland or closely spaced islands may also concentrate and accelerate the tidal flow, particularly when combined with a shelf of shoal water. This can accelerate the tidal flow so violently that it becomes a race, producing an unpleasant series of closely spaced waves, which are at their most chaotic and violent when the directions of wind and tide are opposed. The headland may also feature a mass of underwater rocks, which produce equally violent overfalls. Further problems can occur when a headland produces a reverse eddy that sends the tidal flow back in the wrong direction as it rebounds off the next part of the coast.

The direction and strength of the wind can also have a marked effect on tides. Strong winds combined with low barometric pressure can play havoc with tide heights and times, but of more concern to sailors is the effect of wind against tide. When the wind blows in the same direction as the tide it will calm the waves and make for a smooth passage. However, when the tide turns and flows against the wind, the combination of strong wind and fast flow can push up an ugly series of tightly packed waves. In such conditions sailing against the tide is likely to be a long and unpleasant process, while sailing with the tide could resemble a scary roller-coaster ride.

Go Carefully

Yacht or keelboat sailing is as safe as you choose to make it. For sure there are many potential hazards, but these can be avoided if you think ahead, take plenty of care and accept that you have embarked on a process of continuous education. Accidents may happen and emergencies may occur, but the well-prepared sailor will always be able to minimize the danger through the use of practical common sense as well as knowledge.
• Never sail on your own until you are suitably experienced. If you are alone, always wear a harness and hook on in the cockpit or on deck.

• Avoid sailing after sunset until you are confident about identifing navigational lights and lights on other vessels.
• Get a reliable weather forecast before you leave and regular weather updates. Don't overestimate your abilities. If the conditions don't look right, be prepared to postpone the trip or make for shelter.
• Consult charts and tide tables. Make sure you know where, when and how fast the tides are flowing.
• Avoid any fast flowing tidal race (dangerous tidal flow), and ensure that you can identify underwater obstructions such as rocks and sand banks, which may be covered at high water.

• When sailing in the open sea, always keep clear of shipping lanes and commercial vessels.
• Learn the Rules of the Road and ensure that you abide by them, but don't assume everyone will possess the same knowledge or have the same common sense or manners.
• Beware of the effects of cold and tiredness, which are cumulative unless you take immedate action.
• Drink plenty of liquids when sailing on a hot day. The effects of dehydration are marked.
• Before leaving, always brief your crew on all safety equipment on board the boat.

INSURANCE

As sailing areas become more crowded and attract too many inexperienced people, the risk of collision grows. Hitting and injuring a swimmer or running into another boat and causing damage could result in litigation, and it is vital to ensure that at the very least you have sufficient cover for third party liability.

In some cases a household insurance policy will provide adequate cover, but it may be preferable to seek out a specialized keelboat insurance policy that will operate on a number of levels with premiums tailored to the value of the keelboat and associated equipment. The most important aspects of a specialist policy might include:

Third party liability The most vital component, with a comparatively cheap premium as a stand-alone policy. The amount of cover is tailored to satisfy all legal possibilities.

Liability cover while racing This is mandatory when taking part in most organized events.

Accidental damage cover Normally subject to a policy excess. A specialist insurer should be able to evaluate the claim fairly, help arrange repairs and speed up the entire process.

Accidental cover while racing As for the previous.

ABOVE **Rescue by the Coastguard or Lifeboat is a free service with no calls likely to be made on your insurance, but total cover is still vital to ensure safe, stress-free sailing.**

Cover for theft Normally subject to a policy excess. Check that the cover is sufficient for associated equipment such as clothing, which can sometimes cost almost as much as the boat itself and is easily stolen from a sailing club changing room. Be sure to check the insurance requirements as well, which may stipulate keeping the boat in a locked compound or building.

Roadside rescue and recovery Very useful if the wheels of your trailer decide to seize up due to too much salt water, but this may be covered by your motor insurance policy.

Worldwide cover If you plan to tow your boat abroad, ensure that it has sufficient cover for the relevant countries.

Fire damage A rare occurrence with a sailing boat, but occasionally the result of vandalism.

Medical expenses and transfer These are useful features if you are not already covered by a household insurance. Note the maximum amount of cover being offered.

Dealing with an incident

If you are involved in an incident that is likely to lead to a claim, don't waste time and effort getting angry with the other party. Ensure that everyone is safe and that there is no imminent danger. Be as courteous and logical as the conditions permit, and make a sensible appraisal of both the incident and the damage. Record the time, date and place, take notes and, if possible, make a sketch showing details such as direction of boats, wind speed and direction and conditions on the water. Take a photo of the damage if you can.

Find witnesses to the incident and note down the relevent addresses and sail numbers/boat names for all concerned. Lastly, do not forget to exchange insurance information with the other party involved in the incident. Contact your insurance company at once and deal with sailing experts preferably. Be honest and truthful with your claims.

ABOVE **When a mass of crew are engaged in sailing a high performance boat with associated high risks, it's important to ensure that everyone is covered against accidental injury.**

Basic sailing rules

It is vital to know the rules of the road when sailing. If you don't, your attitude is akin to someone driving on the wrong side of the road. The basic right-of-way rules are comparatively simple, unlike racing rules, which can become incredibly complex and deserve a book (of which there are many) in their own right.

Port gives way to starboard Nothing could be clearer. A sailboat on starboard tack has right of way over all sailboats on port tack.

The windward boat keeps clear If two sailboats meet on the same tack, either port or starboard, the one that is to leeward (downwind) has right of way. This means that a boat that is beating to windward has right of way over a boat that is reaching or running on the same tack.

The overtaking boat keeps clear When cruising, a boat that is behind keeps clear of a boat ahead; a matter of common sense and courtesy. The rule changes somewhat in racing.

LEFT **Whether racing or cruising, the whole purpose of sailing rules is to avoid collisions and ensure that skippers and crews know how to avoid them.**

Keep to the right in a channel This applies to all powercraft and should be borne in mind by small sailboats. In some cases it may be safe and feasible for sailboats to tack from side to side in a channel, but they must leave plenty of space for all craft that need to use the main deep water area and are best advised to keep to the shallower water at the sides.

Right of way rules cover all sailing craft, but they sometimes need to be overruled by common sense. It is a courtesy to give way to a yacht that is

racing when you are cruising, but not mandatory. The racing yacht has no right to force a passage if you have right of way. But, if you meet a large yacht in your small sailboat, it is often much easier for you to give way.

Don't stick rigidly to "power gives way to sail" either. There are times when it is easier for a small sailboat to give way. Some powerboat drivers show little regard or respect for sail, which could lead to tragic consequences if a sailboat insists on enforcing its rights.

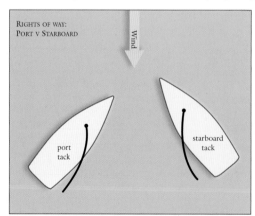

ABOVE **Port must always give way when crossing tacks. In this instance the port tack boat can either tack on to starboard, or bear away below the stern of the starboard tack boat.**

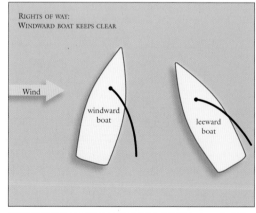

ABOVE **When boats are on the same tack, port tack in this instance, the boat that is on the side the wind is coming from must alter course to keep clear of a boat that is sailing higher.**

RIGHT **Racing rules make overtaking a more complex affair, and rely on the inside boat gaining an overlap before it reaches the turning mark.**

RIGHT **Racing rules make overtaking a more complex affair, and rely on the inside boat gaining an overlap before it reaches the turning mark.**

Rules definition

The use of the rules of the road depend on where your boat is positioned at the time of an incident, what it is doing, where it is going and what is in the way.

Position A boat may be clear ahead, clear astern or have an overlap. This can be determined by running an imaginary line from the stern and bow, set at right angles to the centreline of the boat. If another boat crosses either line, there is an overlap. If no boat crosses either line, your boat is either clear ahead or clear astern.

Movement Many of the rules refer to a type of movement or change of course.

- Luffing is altering course towards the wind.
- Tacking is from the moment a boat is beyond head to wind until she has borne away to a close hauled course.
- Bearing away is altering course away from the wind.

- Gybing is from the moment the foot of a boat's mainsail crosses the centreline with the wind aft, until she completes her gybe when the mainsail has filled on the other tack.

Something in the way An obstruction is any object that is large enough and close enough to require a boat to make a substantial alteration in course to pass to one side. This could include buoys and anchored vessels.

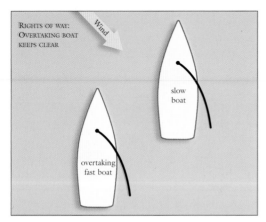

RIGHTS OF WAY:
OVERTAKING BOAT
KEEPS CLEAR

Wind

slow boat

overtaking fast boat

ABOVE **Overtake to either side without forcing the slower boat to alter course. You cannot barge another boat from behind. Overtaking to windward, as shown here is generally the easiest way to get past.**

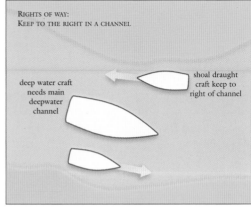

RIGHTS OF WAY:
KEEP TO THE RIGHT IN A CHANNEL

deep water craft needs main deepwater channel

shoal draught craft keep to right of channel

ABOVE **Boats with shallow draught must not obstruct deep water craft, which have priority in a channel. Always be courteous and sensible, and be prepared to give way to larger craft whether under sail or power.**

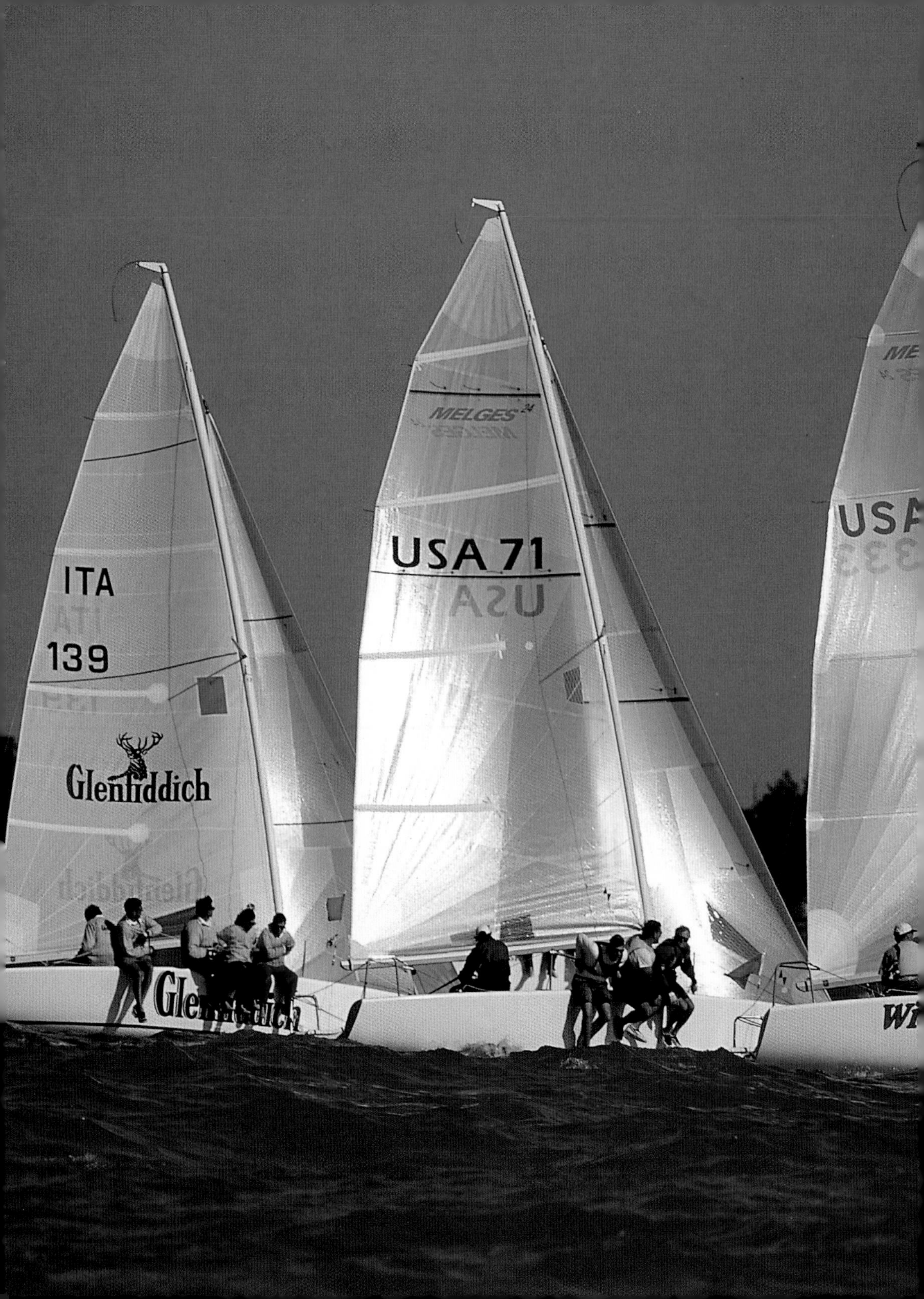
ITA
139
Glenfiddich
MELGES 24
USA 71
USA
Glenfiddich

Keelboat
Basics

Yachts that have ballast hanging beneath the boat come in all shapes, sizes and styles. The keel is there to ensure that they cannot capsize – except in rare and extreme circumstances – and the levels of performance range from sedate cruising to blue ocean racing. Pure cruisers and cruiser-racer yachts comprise by far the biggest category of keelboat, with out-and-out racing boats such as W60 round-the-world racers only accounting for a very small but highly publicized sector. In contrast to the spartan demands of pure racers, cruising yachts aim to combine the best possible accommodation with excellent seakeeping and performance, as do many yachts that can be cruised or raced with equal enjoyment.

An important sub-category among keelboats consists of the smaller open racing boats, many of which have become classic designs, epitomized by the beautiful Dragon, Etchells and Soling, which are all designed for a three man crew. Sportsboats provide a newer thrill in racing keelboats, needing four or five crew to handle a vessel that behaves like a performance dinghy.

Types of keel

The traditional full-length keel has been almost totally superseded by variations on the fin keel. This removes the after part of a full length keel, leaving the ballasted equivalent of a dinghy daggerboard to provide the necessary righting moment and resistance to leewards side-slip, and is likely to offer the best performance in all its forms.

The more performance-oriented the yacht, the deeper and narrower the fin profile is likely to be since hydrodynamic force is proportional to the area of the keel. However, a deeper, narrower fin may prevent the yacht from sailing and mooring close inshore. Drying out on the bottom when the tide goes out is particularly difficult, and the boat is likely to be more sensitive under sail. Most cruising yachts will therefore compromise with a shoal (shallow) draught fin keel, which provides a high level of stability combined with a long, straight bottom for the yacht to rest on. This type of keel is frequently used with a skeg – a mini keel at the back of the yacht that helps balance the rudder.

Bulb and fin keels

These combine a slim, narrow keel with a large lump of ballast fixed to the bottom. This may appear to be a good solution for

LEFT **Even under perfect conditions, careful preparation and a basic knowledge is needed to ensure that cruiser sailing is safe and enjoyable.**

maximizing the righting moment of the keel due to having all the ballast on the tip, but the bulb offers poor performance compared to a tapered fin when it comes to cutting through the water with minimum resistance and maximum lift.

A bulb and fin profile is sometimes used for lifting keels, which retract into the

hull. The fin lifts into a housing inside the boat and the bulb lies flush under the hull to minimize draught.

The disadvantage is the complex mechanical or hydraulic lifting system and a keel case that takes up considerable room inside the boat. Apart from being able to lift the weight of the keel into the hull, the

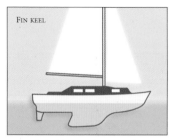

ABOVE **The traditional long keel yacht tends to be very stable, but more slow and ponderous than a fin keel yacht.**

ABOVE **A fin keel that is similar to a dinghy daggerboard gives a yacht maximum performance with very sensitive handling.**

ABOVE **This W60 round the world racing yacht has deep fin keels that provide maximum lift to windward and resistance to leeway.**

design needs to ensure that the keel stays totally rigid and locked down while sailing. A compromise solution is to have a centreboard that lifts into a shallow, stub keel. The centreboard combats leeway and provides lift when fully down and, when retracted, the boat is able to negotiate shoal waters under motor, or possibly under sail with plenty of allowance for leeway and poor response.

Bilge keels

These provide a clever solution for yachts that have to dry out frequently on a mooring or at anchor in tidal waters, and require shoal draught. The identical twin keels protrude from the bilges, and allow the boat to sit upright rather than resting on its side when aground. Due to much greater hydrodynamic resistance the performance of a bilge keeler

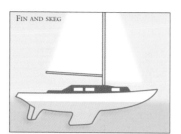

FIN AND SKEG

ABOVE **The fin and skeg is a popular modern compromise, which effectively removes most of a long keel, but retains the after part as a skeg to enhance stability and ensure the rudder remains well balanced.**

is inferior to a yacht with a single fin keel, but cruising performance may be more than adequate when only a small percentage is lost in terms of absolute speed and pointing ability.

BULB KEEL

ABOVE **A torpedo shaped bulb on the end of a fin keel helps concentrate the centre of gravity lower down, allowing stability to be combined with a comparatively short keel for shoal draught sailing.**

LEFT **This Dufour yacht has a large bulb at the end of its short keel with plenty of weight to ensure maximum righting moment and stability. The bulb is extended towards the stern to produce a sufficiently long base for the yacht to dry out in tidal areas.**

LEFT **The bilge keeler provides unrivalled stability when drying out in a tidal location, with two stubby keels resting on the bottom and the ability to sail or motor into shallow anchorages. The downside is that performance is compromised due to the much greater wetted surface area.**

Capsize impossible?

The ballasted keel of a keelboat ensures that it cannot capsize in a conventional sense like a dinghy. The more the boat heels, the more effective the righting moment of the keel becomes, until there comes a point where it is impossible to heel any further. However, in extreme cases a keelboat may be knocked flat on the water by the combined effects of wind and waves. Thankfully this is a rare occurrence. Early problems with open racing keelboats and sportsboats filling with water have largely been solved by the use of self-draining cockpits and better buoyancy distribution. Even short-handed yachts that get knocked down while racing through the Southern Ocean tend to remain afloat even when they lose their keels and turn turtle.

ABOVE **This knock-down on a Hunter 707 looks horrific. However, the centre of gravity has swung in an arc, which takes it further and further from the centre of buoyancy, and it is impossible to tip any further. Only the spinnaker is holding it down.**

Cruiser size

Bigger is better is not necessarily true of yachts where big will almost certainly entail proportionally greater expense in the costs of buying the boat, annual maintenance and everyday running. Additional disadvantages include not being able to get into anchorages, which are delightful but small, due to length or draught, plus the hassle and effort of signing on extra crew to sail the boat. It's not much fun for a husband and wife with two young children to have to manage everything on an 18m (59ft) boat, where big starts to mean heavy and hard to handle.

The obvious advantages of going big are that you get far more space both on deck and below deck with the possibility of large, double berth cabins; the boat will probably go faster due to its extra waterline length; and there is plenty of scope for on-board luxuries such as a fridge, central heating, computer and TV.

However, on top of being cheaper to buy, smaller cruising yachts have a lot going for them. They are cheaper and

LEFT Racing yachts of this size demand a crew that is 12 or 13 strong. Running them becomes a complex management task, which demands considerable expense.

simpler to own, as well as sail, and will often enable those on board to experience a style of sailing that gets as close as possible to the pure sensation of a dinghy. Luck with the weather may be required to enjoy cruising in company on a small yacht, but it is likely to be far more important to keep the boat ship-shape and prevent the depressing build-up of cramp conditions caused by clutter.

6m (20ft) cruisers

This is about as short LOA (length overall) as you can go for comfortable cruising. Two good friends can have a great time if the weather is fine, especially if they have a cockpit tent to provide extra shelter in rainy weather. Facilities for cooking and personal hygiene are likely to be very basic, but a small cruiser of this size should be easy to handle and, if fitted with a lifting keel, will be able to get right into the beach and go where larger yachts dare not follow. Auxiliary power is likely to be provided by oars or an outboard motor.

LEFT **Big is magnificent, but comes at a price. This purpose built 32m (105ft) record-breaking catamaran** Playstation **is very fast, expensive and not practical for everyday use.**

BELOW **Less impressive for sure, but a simple, small yacht can give a great deal of hassle-free pleasure. The most important ingredient may well be the sun, with fair or foul weather making all the difference to the level of enjoyment when sailing.**

RIGHT The Dragonfly 800 trimaran provides a great deal of space for fair weather sailing, with wide trampolines between the main hull and floats on both sides. It also has cracking performance, with no need for a heavy yacht keel owing to the stability of its platform.

LEFT The Bavaria 46 provides all the luxuries a larger yacht offers with a teak deck and sun awning for use in the Caribbean or Mediterranean, while roller reefing headsails and mainsail help ensure it can be handled by a family size crew.

6–9m (20–29¹/₂ft) cruisers

The tendency for designers to produce small cruisers with all the characteristics of a caravan – maximum accommodation with awful looks and even more awful sailing performance – has thankfully been overcome and replaced by more thoughtful creations. A modern yacht in the middle of this range should accommodate up to four adults in comfort on a one or two-week cruise, while a 9m (29¹/₂ft) boat could possibly accommodate up to six adults. In both cases this presumes fine weather – if it is foul and freezing and the crew are forced to spend a lot of time below deck, it will be wise to reduce their numbers by one or two.

Most modern yachts from about 7.5m (25ft) upwards will feature a reasonable fixed galley with a small sink and two-burner stove, a heads (lavatory) compartment complete with a door for privacy, and may also have a fixed navigation area. Boat handling will become progressively heavier as the size of the boat increases and inboard diesel engines take over from outboards as the preferred auxiliary option.

9–14m (29¹/₂–46ft) cruisers

Yachts in this range can pack in a lot of extra space, which is often used to provide double berth cabins and complete owners' suites. Everything is on a bigger scale and include luxury fittings such as ovens, fridges, hot and cold pressurized running water and heating. The galley, heads compartment and navigation centre become progressively grander as the general level of comfort increase, but eight adults on a cruise for an extended period may still feel like a crowd despite the increased size of a 14m (46ft) boat. The rig, sails and anchor also become larger, and are consequently heavier and more difficult to handle. Heavy duty winches are needed to wind up and wind in the sails, and an electric windlass to let down and pull up the anchor.

14m (46ft) plus cruisers

At this level a yacht passes what many people might consider a sensible size for a family cruiser used for coastal pottering. It enters the realm where size may help to make long distance sailing and ocean passages an enjoyable possibility, presuming the crew are experienced and have a yacht that is well set-up for the task in hand.

Wheel or tiller?

Tillers are normally found on smaller cruisers 9m (29¹/₂ft) or less in length where they are a simple, low cost solution to steering the boat. The tiller gives direct feedback from the rudder, which must be balanced so the tiller stays light in the helmsperson's hands with no excess weather or lee helm. The main disadvantage is that the tiller sweeps across the cockpit and uses up valuable space.

Wheels are likely to be standard on any cruiser much bigger than 10.5m (35ft), either fitted with a cable linkage or a hydraulic mechanism, which makes steering easier on bigger yachts. The wheel leaves an uncluttered cockpit for the crew, and enables the helmsperson to change position, steering from either side, or in the middle where he or she can watch the compass. Apart from greater cost, a possible disadvantage is that a wheel system is more complex and therefore more likely to fail than a tiller. An emergency tiller should therefore be carried at all times.

ABOVE The X-412 aims to combine top performance with cruising luxury. Note the roomy and well protected cockpit, stern ladder for swimming and boarding, and wide teak decks comfortable for bare feet (but don't risk bare toes when sailing).

ABOVE When a yacht heels the rudder will pull to windward, and a geared wheel is necessary for comfortable control on mid-size yachts and upwards. The bigger the wheel the better the leverage and response. The helmsman of the Corel 45 has a fine view forwards standing to windward.

Types of rig

The rigs on the majority of modern yachts follow the Bermudan sloop format, either fractional or masthead. In addition there are still plenty of traditional yachts fitted with a wide range of delightful rig variations, which may be less practical, but seldom fail to delight the eye.

Traditional style

A gaff, gunter or lugsail rig may look very fine but, when compared to a modern sloop rig, is likely to be heavier, have more windage and drag, be considerably less efficient upwind and probably more difficult to handle. A possible plus-point is that a shorter mast is required, which, with a quickly lowered gaff, is a useful feature for sailing on rivers with low bridges.

Mizzen style

Yawls and ketches have a mizzen mast and sail aft of the mainsail. This mast is either sited behind the helm (yawl) or in front (ketch), and in most cases is considerably smaller than the forward mainmast. The exception is a two-masted schooner on which the mizzen mast is taller, and therefore becomes the mainmast supporting the mainsail.

The object of a mizzen is to produce a rig that is more balanced fore and aft, with an overall reduction in sail and spar size for easier handling, particularly in very windy conditions when the boat can

LEFT **Wooden boom, mast and blocks add to the weight of a vintage racing rig, with the complexity of running backstays (windward side on the right) to hold it all up.**

be sailed without the mainsail. The principal drawbacks are lost deck space taken up by the extra mast and sail, plus considerable extra cost and complexity. As such the concept is only likely to be

found on very large yachts of 27m (88½ft) and more, where it is desirable to reduce the height of the mainmast and sails and constraints of cost and space are less likely to matter.

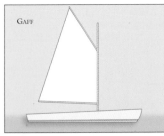

GAFF

GUNTER

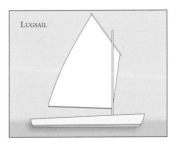

LUGSAIL

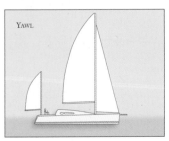

YAWL

KETCH

RIGHT The fractional rig also allows controlled mast bend which is used to vary the amount of camber in the mainsail of a racing yacht as well as tightening the forestay and headsail luff.

ABOVE **The Sunsail Venezia 42 catamaran has an easily handled, fractional Bermudan sloop rig complete with roller furling headsail, making it an ideal yacht for Caribbean charter.**

Sloop style

The Bermudan sloop rig with a single main mast and a sail wardrobe built round two principal sails – mainsail and headsail/jib – is the number one choice for most modern sailboats including dinghies and keelboats of all kinds. Heavy wooden masts have been totally replaced by lightweight, tapered aluminium (and occasionally carbon) masts. High aspect rigs, which do not compromise performance or safety when a boat is heeling or pitching, have been developed. These use sails that can be reduced or increased in area with relatively little effort in order to match changing wind conditions.

There are two principal types of sloop rig. The more traditional masthead rig has a forestay that goes right to the top of the mast and can be used with a full-height genoa. This is suitable for most cruising requirements, but in many cases has been superseded by the fractional rig in which the forestay only goes a certain height up the mast. The fractional rig is a direct development from dinghy sailing and dedicated cruiser racing and has a number of plus and minus features that sets it apart.

The fractional format allows a smaller section, lighter mast, which can be bent or straightened, making the sail flatter or fuller for different conditions. It has the potential for far superior windward performance than a masthead rig, as well as being lighter and more aerodynamically efficient. However, the lighter and bendier the mast is, the more complex the rigging will need to be to prevent it from failing. It may also require considerable input and skill from the crew, who will use the combination of top and bottom runners (running backstays), adjustable backstay and kicker to progressively bend the mast and flatten the sail to their requirements, while maintaining a taut forestay for maximum pointing ability. The additional cost of a high performance fractional rig will of course be considerable, and the concept is not recommended for relaxed cruising.

SLOOP MASTHEAD

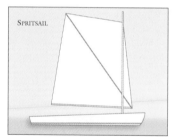

SPRITSAIL

SLOOP FRACTIONAL

SCHOONER RIGGED YACHT

LATEEN

STANDING RIGGING

The standing rigging, which holds the mast up, is generally made of cable using twisted wire strands. The greater the number of wire strands the more flexible the cable becomes. A cable with 259 strands of 0.5mm (¹⁄₅₀in) wire bends so easily that it can be used for applications such as runners and be pulled around blocks, but because the strands are thin they will wear through. At the other end of the scale a cable with 19 strands of 1.14mm (¹⁄₂₀in) wire is very strong, relatively cheap and ideal for straight pull applications such as stays and shrouds. A single strand 8mm (¼in) rod with a smooth outer surface is lighter and more aerodynamically efficient but is generally considered an expensive solution for fixed shrouds, which only racing boats need indulge in.

Sail inventory

A typical cruising yacht might carry the following sail wardrobe:

Mainsail Slab reefing is most common on small to mid-size cruisers. Sail size is reduced by pulling equivalent points on the luff and the leech down onto the boom.

Boom roller reefing is a more old-fashioned option. The sail is rolled around

LEFT **Standing rigging on a Trintella 51, which sports a fairly complex rig with triple spreaders and running backstays to allow a comparatively slim and lightweight mast.**

RIGHT **Bottlescrews allow precise adjustment of the length of the shrouds and inner stays, which help control mast bend. Tape is used to cover the ends of split pins to prevent snags and tears.**

the boom to reduce sail area, but normally sets very poorly due to insufficient leech and foot tension.

Mast roller reefing is a highly sophisticated system mainly used on large, luxury yachts. To reduce sail area the mainsail is wound onto a roller inside the mast. This produces an efficient sail shape with plenty of leech and foot tension, but the mechanics for rolling the sail are complex and expensive.

Headsails Genoas have the clew behind the shrouds when sheeted hard in, and may be either a number 1 (large) or a number 2 (small). Jibs have the clew in front of the shrouds when sheeted hard in, and may also come in different sizes: number 1 (also known as the working jib), number 2, and so on as they get smaller. A storm jib is for use in severe gale force conditions. It is the smallest possible headsail, cut from the same heavyweight

cloth as a mainsail and has robust reinforcement and fittings, with a very short chord and high clew almost halfway up the sail to ensure the flattest possible shape. Modern storm jibs may be coloured bright orange for maximum visibility.

Many cruising yachts are now fitted with a genoa mounted on a roller in the pulpit, which allows the size of the sail to be progressively reduced by roller-reefing. This eliminates the need for filling the interior of the boat with bulky, heavy sails, and is much simpler, and often safer, than sending crew up onto the foredeck to change sails. However, as the size of the headsail is reduced it may progressively loses its shape, becoming baggy and inefficient to windward. Therefore many yachts with roller-reefing genoas carry a separate storm jib to ensure they can make ground to windward in severe conditions.

ABOVE **An in-mast mainsail system allows the mainsail to be rolled into the mast for reefing or total stowage. It is most often used in a powered application on luxury yachts. In some instances the mainsail is rolled inside the boom.**

RIGHT **The overlapping genoa is the powerhouse of most modern high performance yachts. The slot funnells the wind over the leeward side of the mast and mainsail to help drive the rig forwards.**

LEFT The asymmetric cruising chute is, by comparison with a convention spinnaker, an extremely easy sail to use, based on similar principles to the dinghy gennaker but without the same connotations of high performance.

ABOVE Spinnakers always look great and can be a lot of fun to sail with. However, if the wind's up, they demand commitment and skill, with the wide top half of this powerful sail taking over control of the yacht when the crew gets things wrong.

Spinnakers The conventional spinnaker is a relatively complex sail to use, which demands a high level of expertise from the crew and enough spare hands to manage the sheet, guy, pole, hoist and drops.

For cruising use the spinnaker has therefore been superseded by the asymmetric cruising chute, which requires

ABOVE The spinnaker on a racing yacht is launched off the foredeck. The crewman wears a harness, ready to go up the mast or out to the end of the spinnaker boom if required.

no pole, and is flown from a tack-strap with a permanent clew in the style of a dinghy gennaker. The cut of the sail normally combines radial head panels with horizontal lower panels to maximize how easily the sail floats or flies with the wind, and thanks to a dousing sock (a sausage-shape bag that pulls up and down over the sail) the sail can easily be launched and dropped by a short-handed crew.

Materials Woven polyester cloth has long been the favoured material for cruising sails, with heavier cloth up to 23g (1oz) used for mainsails and stormsails and progressively lighter cloth down to 13g (½oz) for genoas and other headsails.

The rapid development of lightweight laminates for racing sails has had an indirect effect on the cruising market, where laminate sails can claim several advantages over woven polyester despite the considerable extra cost:

- Laminates are lighter, which makes them easier to handle, and to a minor extent creates less heel and pitching.
- Laminates are more stable with less stretch. They can be carried higher up the wind scale, and are likely to maintain their shape better when used with a furling system.
- Laminates claim similar durability, if they have woven polyester bonded to both sides of the reinforced scrim for maximum protection.
- Cruising spinnakers and asymmetric chutes are generally made from woven nylon. The best materials combine optimum tear strength, stability and light weight.

What is a laminate?

A traditional polyester sail is made from a solid mass of woven cloth. A laminate sail is made from a layered sandwich of materials, which at its most basic will consist of an open lattice-shaped scrim of fibres held together with resin, with a layer of film bonded to each side. The film prevents air blowing straight through the laminate, the load is taken by the scrim, and the result is a sail material that can be considerably lighter and less prone to stretch than woven polyester, but with greater cost and poorer long-term durability.

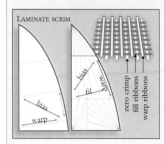

ABOVE A laminate scrim uses bonded warp and fill ribbons, which lie completely flat, to provide maximum resistance to stretch and loading in both horizontal and radial cut sails. Materials used may range from an economical polyester such as Dupont Dacron to top performing High Modulus Twaron combined with Spectra.

Ropes and hardware

Winches, blocks, cleats and ropes all contribute to making it possible for a short-handed crew to handle a relatively powerful rig in safety. With modern design and technology, ropes and hardware are also becoming lighter, more powerful and more efficient.

Ropes and lines

All modern ropes have a synthetic fibre base and are supplied in various diameters that are suitable for specific breaking loads. There are four principal applications listed as follows:

Sheets These need to be easily handled, soft on the hands, flexible and non-kinking. Rope diameter for cruising use will range from about 10–16mm (around ½in) for mainsail and headsail sheets depending on the size of yacht, and upwards from 8mm (¼in) for spinnaker sheets. Colour coding helps to differentiate between spinnaker and headsail sheets and other control lines.

Halyards and control lines These need the best possible strength-to-weight ratio with minimum stretch. They should be non-kinking and easily coiled, with colour coding as well to help differentiation. Rope diameter is likely to range from 8mm (¼in) and upwards.

Anchoring and mooring lines These should be soft and flexible on the hands and non kinking. When choosing lines, suitability for splicing and good abrasion resistance are added factors to look out for. The breaking load of anchoring and mooring lines should relate directly to the displacement (weight of water displaced by a floating boat, same as that of the boat) of the yacht.

General purpose lines These include narrow diameter lines for uses such as burgee halyards, leech lines, outboard starter cords and whipping twine.

Rope care

- Ensure ropes are correctly sized for all deck hardware.
- Make regular checks for chafing against rough surfaces.
- Beware of sharp edges on blocks, cleats, winches and other hardware.
- Ropes should be periodically hand-washed with mild soap to remove salt crystals.
- Unlaying (coming apart) of rope ends can be prevented by applying quality whipping twine or tape.
- Damaged rope must be completely replaced, or where possible cut out and spliced with a new section.

ABOVE **Winches, cleats, clutches and tracks have been designed for minimalist simplicity on the racing yacht Arbitrator, ensuring the weight of hardware is kept to a minimum and is centred in the boat, with plenty of open space for the crew to work at maximum efficiency.**

LEFT The running rigging of a yacht relies on a wide range of modern synthetic ropes, which have been designed for specific applications. While these ropes are very tough, the crew should make regular checks for abrasion, which is bound to occur at stress points.

Rope safety

Beware of rope burn. Never let a rope run quickly through an unprotected hand. Any rope with a synthetic content is potentially dangerous; the cheap kind of floating, brightly coloured nylon rope that fishermen use is the most dangerous of all. If a rope wants to run, take a turn round a cleat to hold it quickly or let it go.

When handling rope, it makes sense to wear protective sailing gloves with reinforced palms that grip well and provide an important level of protection.

Rope clutches

The rope clutch (spin lock) is a unique rope holding system that has superseded the use of cleats for many applications in racing and cruising yachts. The clutch allows the line to be pulled in under load, and the line will lock firmly in position immediately the pulling stops. When there is no load the clutch can be unlocked to let the line run free, and on many designs the clutch will also allow controlled release when the line is at full holding load.

Rope clutches are particularly useful for halyards and control lines such as the outhaul, cunningham, topping lift or genoa furler, and can be used for virtually every cruising application with the exception of headsail and spinnaker sheets.

The clutch is a mechanical device, and care needs to be taken to ensure that it functions correctly. A regular flushing through with fresh water will prevent the build-up of corrosive salt, and small applications of silicone or Teflon lubricant occasionally will help the release action of the axle handle.

Rope slip

This is an occasional problem with clutches; probable causes include:

- The load is in excess of the amount the clutch was designed for. Beyond that amount the clutch will automatically slip rather than damage and possibly break the rope.
- The line is the wrong size or too soft for the clutch. All clutches are designed to operate with specific rope sizes. If the line is smaller, the maximum holding load will be reduced. A top quality hard-cored line will always hold better than a soft-cored line with a loose cover.
- The cam in the clutch may be worn or unsuitable for a new style of modern rope, but can normally be replaced or upgraded.

ABOVE A mass of rope clutches is used to lock off control lines and free up winches, although this yacht has clearly gone for safety in numbers with such an array of pedestals.

ABOVE Sheets need to be soft and easily handled with minimal stretch. Always use bowlines when attaching sheets to the clew of a headsail.

Winches

Geared winches are required to wind in all ropes with high loadings. A typical small cruising yacht will have two primary winches for the genoa and headsail sheets. As yachts get bigger, additional winches may be needed for other uses such as halyards, mainsheet, control lines, spinnaker controls, runners and in the guise of a windlass for the anchor chain. However, winches are heavy, expensive and can get in the way of your mobility on deck. The secret of a successful deck layout is to keep the number down to an absolute minimum, and ensure that they are carefully positioned and able to serve in a variety of roles.

All winch manufacturers recommend winches for specific uses and loadings. On a medium-size cruiser it is normal to have a couple of small, single-speed winches mounted on either side of the coachroof that are used in conjunction with a battery of clutches for halyards and control lines, plus two larger two-speed primary winches on either side of the cockpit for genoa sheets, which can double for spinnaker sheets or guys. Three-speed winches are

ABOVE **A self-tailing winch has a feeder with adjustable jaws, which grip the rope as it rolls off the drum. It is an extremely useful feature that allows one person to wind and winch, but is slower than having one person wind and a second person pull in the tail.**

available for use on larger yachts, with the option of electric and hydraulically driven winches.

Many cruising yachts favour self-tailing winches that have a feeder and spring-loaded jaws to hold the rope as it is wound in. This makes winching a one-person operation, and the only disadvantage over conventional tailing – in which one person winds while another pulls in the rope hand over hand – is that it is considerably slower.

Winch care

Modern winches are reliable, but periodic maintenance will increase their efficiency and minimize the chance of a breakdown.

• Clean your winches every time you sail in salt water. Simply hose down the winches to flush out any salt which will degrade the grease and corrode the metal structure.

• Make a regular five-minute check on each winch by lifting off the drum and removing the main bearings. Use solvent on a rag to wipe away grease on exposed surfaces, and examine for wear or damage to the pawls and gear teeth. Re-lubricate the bearings and gear teeth before reassembly, using all lubricants sparingly.

Winches are generally constructed using a bronze, one-piece centre stem fitted with stainless steel shafts and gear spindles. A rigid nylon case holds the stainless steel bearings, with bronze gear

RIGHT **"Coffee grinders" are linked under the deck on the racing yacht Nicorette, and can be used to drive a selection of winches with one or two crew winding from either side.**

LEFT **Lifting off the drum of a winch reveals the gear train. Maintenance is comparatively simple and should be undertaken on a regular basis to ensure top performance.**

ABOVE **The mainsheet traveller on the Dragonfly 1000 runs across the back of the cockpit, with the double ended sheet led to self-tailing winches on both sides in case it needs to be freed off in a hurry.**

train and stainless steel pawls to prevent the winch from unwinding. The drum itself can be alloy, which is the lightest option, chrome, bronze or even stainless steel.

A good quality handle makes winding a winch much more pleasant. A heavy, chromed bronze handle with a long arm is much easier to use than a flimsy, lightweight aluminium handle, and is even easier to use with a double grip for both hands fitted with roller bearings. The handle should also have a lock to ensure it stays attached to the winch.

Other hardware

Mainsheet traveller Most yachts are fitted with a mainsheet traveller that fits across the full width of the cockpit or coachroof. This enables the mainsail to be sheeted in and maintain a flat leech when away from the centreline, enhancing performance, helping to keep the boat flat, and removing mainsheet falls from the cockpit area when sailing offwind. The traveller normally comprises a sliding ball car mounted on a track, with control lines led to either side.

Mainsheet block systems A simple cruising application will feature two double sheave (the rollers) blocks. The top block is attached to the boom; the bottom block is attached to the main traveller

ball car, with the tail of the mainsheet led through a jamming cleat. This gives a 4:1 purchase, which is suitable for many sub-9m (29½ft) cruisers. For higher loads a top triple-sheave block will give a 6:1 ratio, with the use of ball-bearing blocks optional for smoother running.

Genoa systems Headsail sheets are usually led through a car. This is a block mounted on a track attached to the side deck, and it can be moved fore and aft to adjust foot and leech tension for different sail sizes.

Most cars are adjustable with a simple pull-push plunger, which locks into holes on the track. It is also possible to adjust the car with control lines led back to the cockpit, but in both cases the sheet will need to be eased to allow the car to move.

Vangs and preventers The boom vang or kicking strap on a yacht will generally use similar size blocks as the mainsheet. It may be fitted with snap-shackles at both ends, allowing the bottom to be clipped to the toe rail when sailing downwind. This helps to prevent the boom from involuntary gybes.

Halyard and control line systems These lines are usually led from the base of the mast to a bank of multi-tasking clutches on the coachroof. They can be routed through stainless steel organizers, which are similar to cassettes holding two, four or six sheaves for the lines to run through.

LEFT **A car-mounted block on a sliding track enables the angle of the headsail sheet lead to be moved fore or aft to allow for different sail sizes.**

Offshore clothing

A challenge for clothing designers and manufacturers is to produce offshore clothing that works as an interactive system. It must be flexible enough to keep you warm and dry in the prevailing conditions, as well as being lightweight, comfortable to wear and quick to dry.

The theory of layering

The layering system comprises three layers: base, mid and outer.

Base layer When energy is expended through activity, heat is generated. The body's reaction is to produce sweat. This must be dissipated quickly as it will chill on the surface of the skin, which gets colder faster because moisture conducts heat approximately 30 times faster than air. Dry skin maintains its warmth better than damp skin, thus a base layer worn next to the skin must allow sweat to pass through to the mid and outer layers, without absorbing the moisture or allowing it to return to the skin.

ABOVE **All ready for a wet ride. The W60 Brunel Sunergy shows her pace during the Whitbread Round the World Race, an event where yacht clothing is tested to its ultimate limits.**

OUTER LAYER FOR INSHORE SAILING ....

1 Chest-high trousers are worn over a fleece mid layer and a light base layer.

2 The disadvantage of a smock is that it can be a struggle to put on and take off.

3 Once on, though, it provides a tight, snug fit, which is a lot less bulky than a jacket.

Mid layer Dry skin surrounded by warm dry air conserves body heat, with personal warmth controlled by air insulation. The greater the volume of trapped air there is, then the greater the insulation of the clothing system will be. This is the main function of the mid-layer. It's secondary function is to help transfer moisture away from the body to the outer layer and enable the base-layer to draw sweat away from the skin.

Outer layer This is essentially foul weather gear. By using a breathable fabric, such as Gore-Tex™, the outer layer should be able to exhaust any moisture created inside the system while simultaneously keeping out all wind and water with special waterproof properties and sealed seams, with neck, wrists, ankles and zip (zipper) fastenings completely secure.

Outer layer

Fabric technology has made rapid progress, and materials that combine a totally waterproof finish with breathability are becoming commonplace. This is an important concept for yacht sailing, where long periods of comparative inactivity – sitting in the cockpit or up on the side deck, while dressed against the chilling effect of a cold wind – are interspersed with short periods of intense physical activity.

Tacking, reefing or dousing a spinnaker can all create a lot of body heat in a short space of time, and cold, clammy perspiration may be the result if your clothing cannot breathe. This can be so bad that sailors assume their waterproof jacket or trousers have been leaking, when in fact the problem has come from their own body.

Breathable waterproof clothes will never be 100 per cent efficient. Even if you wear the correct breathable base and mid layers, items such as reflective patches, harness and lifejacket will compromise the efficiency of your outer layer, which cannot rely on conventional ventilation if you are to remain dry. Expense is also a problem, top-rated breathable outer layers sell at prices that may limit their use to those who plan to spend a great deal of time on the water. Occasional cruising sailors may manage almost as well with much cheaper, conventional waterproof clothing.

As a rule, the following features should be found on the very best outer layer clothing:

Jackets

- Flexibility and light weight.
- Bright colours with reflective patches.
- Adjustable storm collar with hood and visor combining precise fit with good visibility.
- Heavy-duty two-way zip (zipper) covered by double storm flap with integral drainage channel.
- Storm cuffs with Velcro adjustable sleeve ends.
- Fleece-lined hand-warmer pockets with storm flaps. (Fleece should be removable for drying.)
- Bellow pockets with mesh drainage and inner zipped pockets.
- Adjustable waist and hip belts.
- Optional integral safety harness.
- Optional integral lifejacket.
- Optional zip-in fleece for extra warmth.

Winding winches is hot work that requires an unobstructed swing of the handle. In marginal conditions, when the risk of waves breaking over the cockpit is negligible, the crew will be much more comfortable without a jacket.

Trousers

- Flexibility and light weight.
- Bright colours.
- Ankle storm cuffs with Velcro adjusters to close over boots.
- No lining for easy entry and exit combined with fast drying.
- Strong, heavy-duty zip with high waterproof gusset.
- Wide elasticized braces plus waist adjustment to keep trousers secure and comfortable.
- Strongly reinforced patches on both seat and knees.
- Chest-high fleece-lined hand-warmer pockets.
- Thick pocket with storm flap and mesh drainage.

ABOVE A lightweight, breathable smock is ideal for small keelboat racing where body movement is at a premium and time on the water is of comparatively short duration.

ABOVE The storm hood has a high, fleece-lined collar, which protects the lower part of the face.

ABOVE For truly extreme conditions with freezing cold, salt water spray, this must be the solution.

CHANGING UP TO A FULL OFFSHORE DRYSUIT ....

1 The offshore drysuit is a heavy duty version of the dinghy drysuit, which may need to be put on rapidly.

2 Internal braces hold up the chest-high trousers at the waist to ensure maximum comfort.

3 Like any drysuit, care needs to be taken pushing hands and feet through the wrist and neck seals.

4 Total protection, but you need a long offshore passage to make this gear worthwhile.

Smock This has the same upper body features as a jacket, but is cut short at the waist with a blouson-style adjustable neoprene waistband to give a more fitted feel and appearance. A blouson therefore looks good, feels less bulky and should be more efficient at keeping the water and wind out. If it is an over-the-head style garment with no front entry zip, it will be considerably more of a struggle to get in and out of, which may be unpleasant down below on a heaving yacht.

Full offshore drysuit This is an extreme garment for extreme sailing conditions – most likely used by round the world sailors. It combines a one-piece waterproof suit with latex neck and ankle seals and integral feet, plus a full-length dry zip across the shoulders. Added to this are the more usual features such as a collar/hood system, ankle and wrist storm closure, reflective strips, pockets and a comfort zip to satisfy calls of nature.

Mid layer

The clothing for this layer is based on synthetic, deep pile, fleece materials such as Polartec, which combine light weight with warmth, breathability and a fast drying capability to give considerably superior performance over natural fabrics such as wool

or cotton. The only real drawback of the material is that it is very flammable, and will melt if touched by flame.

Mid-layer choice is normally divided among jackets, blousons and waistcoats (vests) worn over trousers or salopettes. A fleece jacket or blouson with a rip-stop nylon outer shell will provide sufficient wind- and water-proofing plus durability for times when you don't need to wear an outer layer jacket.

Base layer

This layer is made from a lighter weight fleece than the mid layer, combining maximum wicking with comfort and warmth. The most comfortable and practical solution for sailing is likely to be provided by close-fitting thermal trousers with elasticized waist and ankles, worn with a thermal long sleeve jersey that has a zippered neck to aid insulation and ventilation.

Short-sleeve, turtle-neck and crew-neck variations are all possible, as well as complete one-piece base layer suits.

RIGHT **A heavier duty smock will have similar features to an offshore jacket with storm collar and full hood, but because it has no zip it is likely to be more comfortable for crew work.**

These are theoretically more efficient, but make a considerable addition to the hassle of dressing and undressing on a moving boat.

BUILDING UP THE LAYERS FOR MAXIMUM PERFORMANCE ....

1 A fleece base layer using a material such as Polartec 200 is warm and comfortable, does an excellent job of drawing perspiration away from the skin, and dries quickly when wet.

2 The middle layer may feature trousers or salopettes, using fibre pile or fleece lining to trap the maximum amount of warm, insulating air combined with an outer shell.

3 A jacket or waistcoat completes the middle layer, which can be worn on deck until the weather deteriorates to the point that foul weather gear has to go on.

4 High trousers and a jacket provide the third outer layer, which will provide full protection from wind, rain and cold while sailing.

ABOVE **The three-layer breathable system combines minimum weight and bulk with maximum performance for the crew to function in comfort.**

ABOVE **Windproof clothing and strong sailing gloves for handling synthetic control lines are part of the armoury of modern yacht clothing. This level of gear is ideal for a fresh day when you don't expect to get wet.**

Extremities

Socks Sailing socks should reach well above the shin, stay up with elasticized grippers, and have cushioned soles to provide extra insulation when worn with yachting boots or shoes. Synthetic materials such as polypropylene combine maximum warmth and durability with minimum moisture absorption and are quick drying. Breathable, waterproof socks may potentially be worn for longer without odour, and are there to satisfy the top end of the market.

Footwear Rubber boots need deep cleated soles that grip like limpets and help provide an insulating barrier between your feet and the cold surroundings. Do not wear them ashore any more than you have to, as the alien elements of tarmac and concrete will soon wear down the soft rubber. Boots should have a warm,

comfortable lining, be easy to get on and off but fit well enough to stay on when hanging over the sides of the boat. They must also be light and comfortable when worn for long periods, and provide a snug fit over trousers or under the outer layer. Leather yachting boots, sometimes combined with Gore-Tex™ breathable material, provide a classy alternative for those who want only the best.

Dockside-style leather mocassins are the most popular deck shoes, although some prefer trainer style shoes that provide the same level of grip and protection from

snubbing on uncompromising deck hardware – sailing a cruiser barefoot is seldom a good idea. Some care is needed to preserve leather against the ravages of salt, which may be little more than a hose-down with fresh water. As with yachting boots, the soft soles of deck shoes will wear rapidly if worn ashore.

Headwear About 40 per cent of your body's heat loss can be avoided by wearing the right hat. Nowadays, the simple woolly of yore has been replaced by the modern alternative of a fleece hat, which combines light weight with moisture

ABOVE **Thermal, long sailing socks made from polypropylene yarn provide the right combination of maximum warmth and durability having low moisture absorbency and a quick drying quality.**

ABOVE **Waterproof trousers should fit snugly round boots to prevent water washing up inside. Note the reinforced sides to the boots, which are required for bracing against the toerail and other parts of the boat when moving forwards.**

ABOVE **A fleece-lined waterproof storm cap, which covers the back of the neck, is likely to be an excellent performer. It will keep your head warm and dry, is comfortable to wear and the peak helps deflect spray and sun.**

ABOVE **If it is truly cold, a neoprene balaclava worn beneath an outer layer hood will make a tremendous difference to keeping warm.**

ABOVE **Neoprene-backed gloves with full length fingers will provide good protection for colder conditions, but for exceptionally cold sailing nothing can beat a pair of waterproof and breathable fleece-lined mitts.**

ABOVE **Gloves with short fingers are ideal for easy handling of small diameter control lines, but only in relatively warm conditions.**

resistance and is shaped to grip your head no matter how hard the wind blows. A fleece balaclava worn below an outer layer hood is recommendable for really cold weather, while fleece-lined storm caps do a good job of combining thick warm fleece with a waterproof outer shell and peak, and can even be found in the style of the old fashioned oilskin fishermans's hat.

Gloves and mittens. Modern synthetic ropes and lines can be hard on the hands, and dinghy-style gloves with mesh backs and padded leather palms can be recommended for general use in full-finger and short-finger variations. If the gloves are to provide any cold weather insulation they will need neoprene backs, while the only real answer for serious winter sailing is to wear full length, fleece-lined mitts made from a breathable, waterproof shell fabric with adjustable closure at the wrists.

Fair weather sailing

Always wear shoes on deck when sailing. They grip better than bare feet and you won't damage your toes.

You owe it to your yacht to stay smart. If it's hot, wear shorts and a comfortable T-shirt, polo-shirt or crew-shirt. If it's cooler, crew pants should be made from a quick-dry material, have large useful pockets, and may benefit from knee and bottom reinforcement patches if you can live with a bizarre appearance.

During summer a peaked cap will provide your face with useful protection against the sun, but take care to protect the back of your neck as well. Wear sunglasses to cut out associated glare and prevent possible UVB damage.

Luggage

Invest in the best possible luggage made in a strong coated fabric for maximum water resistance with suitably sturdy plastic zips (zippers). Beware of over-size crew bags, which can be a nightmare to carry. It is better to have two small ones, plus a matching backpack if required. Use a navigator's case or document case to keep all your paperwork together.

LEFT Sailing luggage should be lightweight, durable and water resistant. This style of navigator's case is ideal for taking paperwork on board.

BELOW In fair weather the crew still needs deck shoes to protect their feet and polo shirts to help keep off the sun. Note that the crewman forward is wearing waterproof trousers as the foredeck is likely to take a few waves.

Safety

The sea can be a very treacherous and dangerous place. However, modern equipment and survival techniques help to make it as safe as possible.

LIFEJACKETS

Every yacht should carry enough lifejackets for the number of crew on board. One size should fit most adults, with smaller children's sizes provided as required. The lifejackets should be easily accessible. Every member of the crew should know where they are and practise how to put them on before setting sail. Many cruising sailors will only don a lifejacket for night sailing or rough weather, but it is good practice to encourage crew to wear a lifejacket whenever they go on deck, particularly for those unable to swim.

International regulations

International standard have a number of basic requirements with minor variations. Regulations for Europe are typical:

- A lifejacket must be a distinctive colour.

- The lifejacket should allow freedom of movement on deck and in the water, where there should be adequate head movement without interfering with hearing or breathing.
- Donning a lifejacket should be obvious, simple (except for young children who will require assistance) and not unduly affected by adverse conditions such as poor light, cold or wet.
- The means of adjustment must be obvious and easy to carry out to ensure a secure fit. After reading the instructions printed on a lifejacket, the wearer should be able to don and securely adjust it within one minute.
- Auto-inflation systems must inflate the lifejacket sufficiently to float the wearer within 5 seconds of being triggered. Oral top-ups must be possible when in the water.
- The force required to operate the pull-toggle for the inflator should be between 20 and 120 Newtons (5 to 25lbs).
- A wearer should be able to leap into

ABOVE **A floating strobe light attached to the lifejacket is a useful feature. It will activate as soon as the lifejacket hits the water and inflates.**

the water from a height of up to 1m (just over 3ft) without displacing the jacket, causing injury or effecting its performance.
- The lifejacket must self-right the wearer face-up within 5 seconds, without any voluntary movement. This is particularly important if the wearer is unconscious.
- A lifejacket should provide lateral and occipital (back part of the head) support so the mouth of a well relaxed

ABOVE **The combined harness and lifejacket is neat and comfortable to wear, and not at all bulky. The lungs of the lifejacket are neatly stowed inside the red covers.**

ABOVE **Once inflated by the CO_2 cartridge, the lungs can be orally topped up if required. In most instances they should not be inflated while on the boat, since they will clearly restrict movement.**

ABOVE **The harness should be adjusted for a close but comfortable fit, and be provided with a nylon webbing safety line that has easy-to-use clips at both ends.**

individual is held clear of a still water surface with the trunk of the body inclined backwards at an angle between 30 and 90 degrees.

- A lifejacket wearer should be able to swim 10m (33ft) and easily climb a vertical ladder.
- The wearer must not show any tendency to slip out of the lifejacket while in the water.

Buoyancy

Lifejackets with a buoyancy of 150 Newtons (33lb) are suitable for coastal and offshore uses; 275 Newtons (63lb) is recommended for long-distance passage.

Most modern lifejackets are worn with the air chambers deflated to eliminate cumbersome bulk. Inflation is usually a two-stage process with an automatically fired CO_2 cylinder (one-time use) followed by oral back-up if required. The standard automatic inflation trigger for lifejackets is activated when a salt-water tablet is fully immersed. An alternative hydrostatic system based on water pressure has been introduced to eliminate the possibility of a salt-water tablet activating due to damp or very wet conditions. All automatic lifejacket systems need to be re-armed at specific service intervals.

HARNESSES

A harness must always be worn – and used – when going on deck at night. Disappearing over the side is most likely to occur when a member of the crew goes forward in rough weather, and has to unclip his or her harness to change position. Therefore, if a crew member needs to wear a harness he or she must also wear a lifejacket and vice versa. A combination lifejacket and harness makes good sense, and is faster and less fiddly to put on. If you wear a separate harness and lifejacket, always put the harness on first to ensure it is fully secure.

As with lifejackets, every yacht should carry enough harnesses to fit the number of people on board. They should be easily accessible, with every member of the crew knowing where they are and how to put them on before setting sail.

Yacht basics

Sailing on a yacht can mean anything from a day out with the family visiting a nearby bay, to a round the world tour spread over several years. Most of us are able to experience the former while only dreaming of the latter, for even if you can't afford to own a yacht there is always plenty of demand for crew – and the more experienced the crew, the more rewarding their role will be.

Whatever type of cruise you wish to undertake you must cruise within your capabilities, which includes the following:
- Good planning and preparation.
- A cautious attitude to sailing and cruising that always puts safety first.
- Maintaining a yacht that is tidy and ship-shape at all times.

- Courtesy to other members of the crew, and an understanding of their needs, requirements and concerns.
- Courtesy towards all other vessels, and a precise knowledge of rights of way.
- Sufficient knowledge of navigation (reading a chart, taking a bearing, and understanding weather forecasting and tides).
- The ability to change plans rapidly and decisively to meet changing circumstances, particularly in deteriorating weather.
- A relaxed, confident and knowledgeable attitude to yacht handling, which inspires respect in the crew.

A harness should have an adjustable waistband and shoulder straps, with a front opening stainless steel buckle and robust D-ring for the safety line. The safety line should be made from a 1–2m (3–6ft) length of nylon webbing with a minimum 2080kg (4,586lb) breaking strain, and stainless steel carbine clips at both ends. Some stretch lines incorporate a third hook in the middle.

Get used to moving around the deck with a harness and learn where and what is safe to clip on to. The traditional jackstay – a wire safety cable running along the coachroof or side decks – allows the crew to slide fore and aft and the webbing provides a 1–2m (3–6ft) reach either side. Never clip to the lifelines running between the stanchions, which are comparatively flimsy.

ABOVE **Bashing to windward can be a cold and wet affair. The crew on the lead boat looks vulnerable with deck shoes rather than boots.**

Sailing Techniques
and Classes

Learning to handle a cruiser is rather different from learning to handle a dinghy. You can move around the deck of a cruiser without it tipping over, everything should happen in virtual slow motion (at least while you learn), and there should be absolutely no chance of a capsize. However, the stakes are considerably higher when you skipper a large, sometimes unwieldy and often rather expensive craft, and have the responsibility for a number of crew on board. The subject also becomes considerably wider as it encompasses areas as diverse as marine engines and electronic navigation.

Basic cruiser handling can be learnt in a reasonably short space of time and will open the door to one of the most delightful pastimes. However, knowledge that is learnt so easily is little more than a prelude to a lifetime of gaining experience, and nothing is more important than learning to respect the unpredictable power of the elements. Wind and sea can turn when you least expect it and catch out the expert sailor as readily as the novice, and will continue to do so for as long as we love to sail.

Handling the mainsail

The primary power source of a yacht sailing to windward is the mainsail. This is also the most easily controlled sail on the yacht because it is accessible from the cockpit, and a powerful multi-purchase mainsheet provides relatively quick and effortless adjustment.

Preparation

- Undo the mainsail cover and fold it along the boom, working aft from the mast. Stow in a cockpit locker.
- Free off the main halyard and attach the shackle to the head of the mainsail. Take up the slack, ensuring the halyard is not caught round the shrouds.
- Undo the sail ties. Many modern yachts have a spider made up of a single length of shockcord below the boom with numerous legs that fasten round the sail. If using conventional shockcord ties, be very careful that loose ends do not fly off – serious eye injuries have been caused this way.
- Free off the mainsheet, traveller and kicking strap. Before hoisting, make sure the wind is well forward of the beam, ideally the yacht should point head to wind.

LEFT **Attach the halyard to the head of the mainsail with the shackle, which has a pin that will turn and lock. Make sure the halyard does not lasso the spreaders, and keep it taut at all times.**

TAKING OFF THE MAINSAIL COVER ....

1 Start from the mast, and unclip and untie to the vertical overlap of the cover.

2 From this point you can start to fold the cover back along the boom while you work aft.

3 Lift the shockcords off the hooks as you go along.

4 If the wind takes control you may need another pair of hands.

Hoisting the mainsail

There are various methods of hoisting the mainsail, which one you use will largely depend on the size of sail and how much effort is required to get it up. On a small to medium-size yacht the main halyard will normally be led aft through a clutch on the coachroof, allowing for one crew to stand in the cockpit and pull it in hand over hand.

The helmsperson keeps the yacht head to wind, and may need to keep a hand on the falls of the mainsheet to stop the boom from moving around. While the mainsail is being hoisted, the helm's vision is likely to be drastically reduced. If the yacht is under way a lookout must be kept at all times. The helmsperson should also watch that the batten ends don't catch on lazy-stays (if used) or get caught on the wrong side of the shrouds.

As soon as the halyard starts to feel heavy, it's time to take a turn round the relevant coachroof winch. You can then spin in a few more handfuls of halyard. If a second crew sweats up the halyard – he pulls a triangle of rope outwards from the mast or coachroof which the other crew can then pull in on the winch – it helps get the sail up faster. Once pulling becomes slow and difficult, it's time to wind the mainsail to the top of the mast, which will require three turns round the winch. Either use the self-tailing mechanism, or get another crew person to tail (pull the

LEFT **Undo the sail ties that are used to hold the mainsail in a neat bundle along the boom. Beware of old fashioned shock-cord ties, which can fly round and hit you in the face; beware also of obscuring the helm's vision if you let the sail fall down off the boom.**

ABOVE **The mainsail can be rolled tight to the boom or flaked as shown here. Sail ties are the traditional way of securing the sail, and safer than shockcord ends flailing around.**

rope in hand over hand), which is considerably faster. The halyard should be wound in until the luff appears sufficiently taut. Before pulling in on the mainsheet, the topping lift, which holds the boom up, must be slackend off or removed and taken forward to the base of the mast.

Once the sail is sheeted hard in the kicking strap can be tensioned. Check how the sail sets. Horizontal creases indicate that the luff should be tighter – you will need to free off the mainsheet and kicker to wind up more halyard. Vertical creases indicate that the luff is too tight, and you need to ease the halyard.

Dropping the mainsail

When dropping, the helmsperson's view is likely to be severely obstructed for a few minutes. It is generally safer to drop the mainsail at anchor; if under way, a careful

lookout must be maintained. The wind must be well forward of the beam to drop the sail. The mainsail slides will drop down the track most easily when the yacht is head to wind.

Free off the mainsheet and kicker, and take up on the topping lift to ensure the boom does not drop on anyone's head. It may be necessary to wind in the main halyard to free off the clutch or cleat.

When ready, the crew should be prepared to let the halyard run in a controlled fashion, ensuring there are no snarl-ups in the tail. A second crew may need to pull the slides physically down the track, and start bundling the mainsail into a roll starting at the mast. The crew in the cockpit can then let the halyard run, and jump onto the side deck or coachroof to help roll the mainsail into a bundle that is tight to the boom. At this stage, it is vital

that the helmsperson pulls in on the mainsheet to prevent the boom swinging from side to side. He should also ensure the yacht points into wind so the sail falls between the lazy-stays (if fitted).

The crew removes the main halyard, which should be secured away from the mast to prevent clattering caused by wire cable beating against alloy. Attach the sail ties, put on the sail cover if required, and coil the tail end of the mainsheet to make everything ship-shape and tidy.

Knotting sail ties

Conventional sail ties without a loop can be secured with a reef knot. Learn to get it right; there is a 50:50 chance of tying it the wrong way.

SWEATING UP THE MAINSAIL ....

1 Sweating is a good technique to get the mainsail halyard up fast.

2 One crew pulls a length of halyard out from the mast. The other pulls the slack through the clutch.

3 Winding need only be used to achieve final luff tension.

Handling the headsails

Yachts with conventional headsail systems rely on a choice of headsails to match wind conditions. Minimum requirements are likely to be an overlapping genoa for light to moderate winds, a working jib for moderate to strong winds, and a storm jib for excessive winds.

Many cruisers still use traditional bronze or stainless steel hanks with a piston closure to attach the luff to the forestay. The alternative headfoil system uses a special forestay fitting, which has one or two full length grooves that hold the boltrope of the luff. This is potentially much lighter and aerodynamically more efficient than hanks and, with a double groove, allows two headsails to be hoisted at the same time for fast sail changes when racing. The downside of the headfoil is that it is more prone to damage, and there is limited scope for do-it-yourself repairs while at sea.

In anything more than a light wind, it is generally easiest to hoist or change a headsail offwind. The boat has a kinder motion and is less likely to heel over, while the headsail will be partly blanketed by the mainsail and is less likely to put up a fight.

Hoisting a headsail

Pull the relevant sail bag up on deck. The most direct route may be through the forehatch, but this is not recommended if the boat is under way and pitching with water coming onto the foredeck. Secure the sail bag to the leeward side toerail so it remains inside the guardrail and you can work from the windward side. If there is any question of personal safety, wear a lifejacket and harness and clip on.

Modern headsail bags are shaped like a sausage with a full length Velcro-sealed opening along the side. Locate the tack of the sail and clip it to the snap-shackle tack fitting. If using hanks, start from the bottom hank and work up the luff, ensuring all hanks are the right way up – it's surprisingly easy to twist them through 180 degrees. Push the hanks down the forestay to ensure the sail does not start to fill and blow over the side. If using a headfoil, the head of the sail must be fed into the foil guide, a little metal triangle that feeds in the luff to ensure that it does not jam when the halyard goes up. A headfoil generates greater friction than hanks. Windward and leeward sheets should be attached to the clew with tight bowlines. The sheets are led aft through blocks to the primary winches where figure-of-eight knots secure the ends.

When the crew is ready to hoist, the halyard must be given plenty of slack so the snap shackle can be taken forward and attached to the head. Beware of allowing the halyard to blow back round the spreaders or forward round the forestay. The halyard should be pulled up hand over hand and as fast as possible. Only begin winding when you can pull no more. It is vital that the leeward sheet is free, so the sail doesn't power up before it is fully hoisted. Secure the halyard with the clutch or cleat. Sheet in, and check the sail

ABOVE **Use sail ties to hold the headsail to the guardrails or toerail when not in use. Remove the halyard, clip the end to the pulpit and take up the slack.**

for horizontal or vertical creases, indicating the luff is too slack or too tight. Check the shape of the foot and leech, which should match each other in smooth, flat curves. If the foot is too full, the car on the fairlead traveller needs to be moved aft; if the leech is too full, the car needs to be moved forwards. The sheet must be eased off to accomplish this.

Dropping a headsail

If the yacht is sailing upwind, it may be pitching, heeling and taking waves over the foredeck; all of which can make sail changing a difficult task. In order to remove any potential problems for the crew on the foredeck, the drop must be precisely controlled by the crew in the cockpit.

One crew should let off the halyard, and control the rate of descent so that the headsail doesn't blow over the side and dump in the sea. Keeping the leeward sheet hard in will ensure the sail drops inside the guardrail, but the foredeck crew may need to call for slack if the hanks won't slide down the forestay. If the sail bag is on deck it should be securely attached to the leeward toerail. The foredeck crew bundles the sail as low as it will go on the forestay, before unclipping and securing the halyard, and the cockpit crew keeps enough tension to prevent it blowing around the spreaders or forestay. Let off the hanks from the top, and feed the top of the sail into its bag with the tack going in last and on top. Undo the sheet ends, which can be tied together or onto the pulpit for temporary security, and bundle in the clew end of the sail before closing the sailbag. If it's dry you can

SETTING THE HEADSAILS ON A LUFF FOIL ....

1 Attach the tack by a snap shackle.

2 Loosely flake the sail with the head at the top.

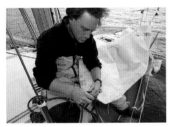
3 Lead both sheet ends to the clew of the sail.

4 Attach the sheets using bowline knots.

5 Tie each bowline tight to the cringle.

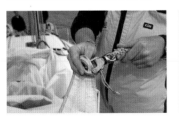
6 Attach the halyard to the head of the sail.

7 Push the top of the bolt rope through the feeder.

8 Pull 1m (3ft) of the bolt rope up the luff foil.

9 Ensure the bolt rope feeds without snagging.

10 Sweat the halyard to help get it up fast.

11 Wind in the halyard for final luff tension.

RIGHT **The winch being used to wind in the headsail has a self-tailing facility, but it is quicker and more powerful if one crew tails by pulling in the sheet hand-over-hand as shown here. The tailer should keep well clear of the winder whose hands whirl round in a 360 degree circle. The tailer should also watch the leech of the headsail, advising on progress and judging when it is time to stop winding.**

bundle the bag below; if it's wet you may prefer to leave it on deck. An alternative is to bag the sail later and leave it secured temporarily to the guardrails by sail ties.

Beware that, when a headsail is being lowered for a sail change, the yacht will lose forward momentum and steerage. Always make sure there is sufficient sea room to allow for leeway and loss of manoeuvrability during any headsail change, when the mainsail may need to be eased to make handling more responsive.

When changing headsails it saves a lot of time if the car controlling the headsail fairlead position is moved to the right place on the track before sheeting in. The track can be marked to show the correct position for each sail.

Using a winch

All winches turn clockwise and the rope is wound round them in a clockwise direction. You should put on just enough turns to hold the rope around the winch without slipping. Any more, and you risk jamming the winch with a riding turn.

When starting to pull in a rope, you just need a single turn round the winch. Any more turns will slow down the process of pulling in and risk a riding turn. Put on

a second turn when the pull of the rope starts to get heavy, followed by a third turn just before you need to insert the handle and start winding. You should always be able to hold the sheet on the winch drum. If it slips, you need another turn.

To ease the sheet use your free hand to physically move the turns round the drum. To remove the sheet completely – as when tacking – take enough turns off the drum so you can just hold the rope, then spin the rest vertically off the drum.

Riding turns If the bottom turn on the winch rides up on the second turn – usually when you have too many turns and are

pulling in hand over hand – it will jam and create a riding turn, which jams the sheet so it cannot be eased off. If you see the bottom turn start to ride up, you should immediately let the turns slip round the drum, which should cure the problem. If you are too slow and the riding turn jams on the winch, the solution is to take tension off the pulling end of the rope and lift the free end straight off the winch.

Using a handle Beware of flailing around with a winch handle while transferring it from winch to winch. It is surprisingly easy to smack a fellow crew member in the face with this uncompromising object.

USING A SELF-TAILING WINCH ....

1 When ready to wind, take enough turns to fill the body of the winch, pulling the sheet over the feeder and round the jaws.

2 Wind in steadily, and the free end of the rope will be thrown clear by the self-tailing mechanism.

It is important to find a comfortable and effective position for winding, where you can swing the handle round its arc with minimum effort, and without hitting fellow crew members with your elbows. The ergonomic design of the cockpit will reflect how efficiently you can wind, as will the weight and length of the handle. A double-handhold delivers the most potential power. Ensure that the winch handle is firmly locked into the top of the drum before you start winding. On a two-speed winch you wind one way for the high gear, then reverse the winding direction for the low gear. The skill is to get the sail sheeted home before you need to use the low gear, and then use its slow speed for fine tuning.

WINCHING TRICKS ....

1 Beware of the riding turn, which will appear if too many turns are put on too rapidly. If it locks solid, the only solution is to remove all the loading.

2 When winding you need a comfortable position and room to swing the handle. How easy it is will also depend on how far the boat is heeling.

Roller-reefing headsails

These combine a luff foil with top and bottom rollers and allows sails to be changed using the same technique as any headfoil system, with the choice of at least one heavy and one light air sail to cover all conditions.

The windier it is, the flatter a headsail needs to be. Roller-reefing systems with tack and head swivels independent of the foil allow the centre of the sail to furl before the tack and head to produce a flatter shape for reefed sailing.

Many owners leave a roller-genoa hoisted for the whole season. A sun cover should be used for protection from the effects of ultra-violet light.

Roller technique Furling and unfurling a roller headsail is essentially a simple operation with a single control line led from the coachroof to the stem-head drum. The line must be fully wound round the drum when the sail is full out, and fully unwound when the sail is full in.

Problems can be caused by the reefing line taking riding turns or dropping off the drum. To prevent this, the line must always be kept under tension.

Never let the reefing line go with a bang if there is enough wind to power up a partly unfurled sail. On any medium-size yacht the line should be eased off from a winch, with careful use of the leeward sheet to encourage the sail to unfurl. When reducing sail in stronger winds, the reefing line will often need to be winched in with the sheet eased off. The reefing line must always be securely held by a self-tailer, human tailer, clutch or cleat.

Reefing the mainsail by rolling it around the boom is relatively inefficient, and has been superseded by slab reefing for both racing and cruising use. The option of rolling the sail inside the mast is reserved for larger, more exotic cruising yachts.

- Always reef early – it is much easier to reef before the going gets tough.
- Make sure the crew know what they have got to do.
- Reefing needs to be done quickly, as the mainsail is prone to damage while it is flogging in a heavy breeze and can be dangerous with crew struggling on deck.

Slab reefing The helmsperson steers the yacht so the wind is forward of the beam. It is difficult to reef if the mainsail is pressed against the shrouds. Mainsheet and kicker must be eased right off, with the topping lift made up so the boom will not drop into the cockpit.

BELOW **The luxurious Wauquiez 43 cruiser boasts twin furling headsails and a mainsail that furls on an internal boom roller for maximum cruiser-friendliness.**

ABOVE **This Harken furling drum clearly shows the strongly engineered, heavy duty nature of a piece of equipment that has to withstand extremely high loads without any chance of failure.**

RIGHT **Despite very light winds, this yacht has its mainsail pulled down to the first reef. It also has the No2 and No3 reefing pennants led through the leech of the sail. These control lines are used to pull the leech down to the outer end of the boom, creating a new clew position for the second and third reefs in the mainsail. On a cruising yacht they can be left permanently in position, which is useful in area such as the Aegean where afternoon winds of Force 6 (22–27 knots) are quite common during the summer.**

One crew takes responsibility for the halyard, which will most likely be controlled from the cockpit. He or she eases the halyard so the foredeck crew can pull the relevant tack cringle down to a hook on the side of the boom – luff slides may need to be removed to accomplish this. The cockpit crew re-tensions the halyard, and pulls the relevant clew pennant tight so the new clew position is hard down and full out along the boom. It is vital that the mainsheet is free when doing this. Finally, the clew pennant is locked off, the topping lift is released, the helm brings the boat back on course, and the mainsheet and kicker are pulled in. Excess sail can be rolled into a tight bundle on the windward side of the boom and tied off as necessary.

Shaking out a reef To reverse the process and take out a reef, the kicker and mainsheet need to be eased off and the topping lift made up. The crew then lets off the tack pennant, and drops the halyard to unhook the tack cringle, before re-hoisting the sail to its full extent.

PUTTING A SLAB REEF IN THE MAINSAIL ....

1 With the topping lift supporting the end of the boom, the cockpit crew eases off the halyard.

2 The foredeck crew has pulled the luff cringle down to the first reef point and takes the halyard.

3 The luff must be fully tensioned using the halyard before the leech can be pulled down on the boom.

4 The No1 reefing pennant pulls the leech down and out along the boom. Excess sail can then be rolled into a tidy bundle secured by sail ties.

Using auxiliary engines

Auxiliary power plays a vital role when manoeuvring in confined spaces, when it is impractical to sail and when charging battery powered electrics.

Inboard engines

Most cruising and racing yachts over about 7.5m (25ft) are fitted with inboard diesel engines. They are practical, reliable and economic to run. In addition, they can be sited low down in the yacht where their weight contributes to the righting effect of the ballast and the propeller will always stay underwater.

Unlike petrol (gasoline) engines, the fuel of diesel engines is not affected by temperature, will not produce explosive vapour and requires no electric spark for ignition, which has the added benefit of making diesel engines considerably more resistant to the effects of damp or water. The safety disadvantages and greater fuel consumption of petrol engines make them a non-starter for inboard use, even though they are lighter and quieter.

Most modern inboard engine installations feature a variation on the Saildrive (see below), which has an integral propeller

ABOVE **An auxiliary diesel engine gives effortless power and control at the touch of a button. It is highly effective in this kind of light wind situation, but the windage on the rig of a yacht may make handling under power considerably more difficult in a strong wind.**

unit sited directly beneath the engine. This is considerably simpler than the traditional full-length propeller shaft, is entirely suitable for fin keel yachts, and tends to make steering more precise and predictable.

Outboard engines

Smaller yachts are sometimes fitted with outboard engines, with 4-stroke power providing a heavier but quieter and

smoother running option than 2-stroke. Outboards are considerably cheaper than inboards to buy and install, and occupy very little space inside the yacht. They can also make the yacht very manoeuvrable if the motor can be moved through 180 degrees to execute tight turns.

Outboards are often fine for auxiliary use at an anchorage or in a marina, but do not provide the consistent performance

RIGHT **The saildrive style of propeller-to-engine coupling was a great step forward, placing the engine directly over the propeller for easier installation and superior handling.**

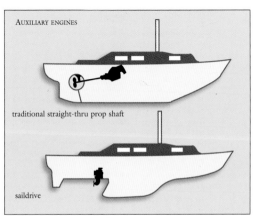

AUXILIARY ENGINES

traditional straight-thru prop shaft

saildrive

ABOVE **On most small or medium-size yachts engine access is behind the companionway ladder, with everything easily to hand for everyday maintenance and excellent sound insulation.**

ABOVE **Multihulls such as the Dragonfly 800 (top) and F-24 (bottom) will generally only use their outboards for auxiliary power when berthing, and mainly rely on pure sail power.**

Diesel engine controls

ABOVE **The instrument panel is located in the cockpit coaming for easy access by the skipper. The combined throttle/gear control (black handle) is shown in the full astern position, and the nearby pull lever is used to stop the engine. Before starting, always ensure the gear button is in neutral.**

Before starting an inboard diesel engine, check there is sufficient fuel, oil and fresh water coolant, and that the salt water inlet and outlet is open.

Most modern diesel engines use a simple key-start, with a push button, puller and/or key stop. The standard throttle and gear control is a combination lever with a central red button for neutral.

- Button in: engine is in neutral, pushing lever forward or back increases revs.
- Button out: engine is in neutral when the lever is only in the upright position.

- Engine is in forward gear with lever in forward position: push to full forward for full revs.
- Engine is in reverse gear with lever in backward position: push to full backward for full revs.

Always pause in neutral when changing from forwards to reverse and vice versa, it's kinder to the gearbox.

Run the engine at no more than half power for a few minutes while the engine is warming up, and before shutting off in order to let the engine cool down. Never run the engine flat out. It will use a lot more fuel for a negligible increase in speed.

required for extended running in adverse conditions. An engine requires an output of 4–5 horsepower per ton of displacement if it is to function as an effective auxiliary. The ultimate test is being able to drive a yacht straight into a strong wind or tide, while maintaining a speed of at least 5 knots. In such conditions an outboard powered yacht may perform better under sail, which removes the additional risk of a wave drowning the ignition.

Most outboards are transom-hung and may need to be sited to one side of the rudder. The propeller may be lifted from the water when the boat heels away from the outboard, with the result that the yacht loses forward momentum. This problem can be exacerbated if the yacht is pitching, or crew have to go on the foredeck. If it is persistent the engine will keep over-revving with possible damage to the transmission. It may also overheat due to the water inlet lifting clear of the water.

On many yachts, dropping and lifting the outboard is a real hassle. The helmsperson has to bend over the transom and fiddle with the motor, looking aft

when he or she should be looking forwards. Left on its transom bracket, the outboard is prone to theft. Lifting it off and locking it away in a cockpit locker is a gut-wrenching operation that can be tricky as you balance on the back of the boat. You should also beware of petrol leaking out of the outboard when it is laid on its side in the cockpit or in a locker, which should be water tight and air tight to contain petrol and its fumes.

An outboard has a limited fuel supply compared to the inboard tank of a diesel. Outboards with integral fuel tanks have the most limited running time, and are difficult and potentially dangerous to refill when under way. A remote fuel tank located in the cockpit or a cockpit locker is a more practical and safer option.

Hot engines

Overheating is a common problem with both inboard and outboard engines, and will become obvious if an audible alarm goes off (fitted on modern diesel engines) or if no cooling water is being pumped from the outlet. The likely cause is a blockage in the sea water inlet, which prevents sea water from being sucked in to cool the sealed fresh water cooling system. Stop the engine, and check for debris.

Mooring and anchoring

Nowadays many yachts are berthed side-on to a floating pontoon or dock in a marina, or have a swinging mooring attached to a buoy. A few yachts may be berthed to a quay or harbour wall, generally in non-tidal areas.

MARINA BERTHING

Most marina pontoons and the yachts alongside them go up and down with the tide in a protected environment. Other marinas have locks and are accessible only a few hours either side of high water. Yachts will normally be secured by the following lines:

- **Bow line** Led forward from a cleat on the foredeck to a cleat, ring or bollard on the pontoon.
- **Stern line** Led aft from a cleat on the aft deck to a cleat, ring or bollard on the pontoon.
- **Springs** Fore and aft springs pull against the bow line and stern line to keep the yacht snug alongside the pontoon without the stern or bow swinging out. They can either be led from the middle of the pontoon to the bows and stern of the yacht, or from the middle of the yacht to equivalent positions on the pontoon.

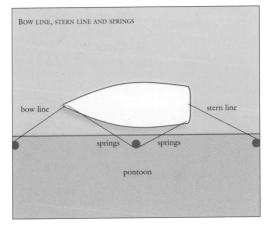

BOW LINE, STERN LINE AND SPRINGS

bow line   stern line

springs   springs

pontoon

LEFT The bow and stern lines hold a yacht fore and aft, with springs to hold it in tight alongside. The springs should be led fore and aft from the middle of the pontoon or quay, as shown, with all lines adjusted so the yacht is aligned alongside with sufficient space for fenders.

Securing the lines

Mooring lines should be led through the appropriate fairleads, which are cut into the toerail. Each line from the yacht may be secured to its cleat by a tight bowline.

A full turn, half turn and locking turn should be used to secure the line to a cleat on the pontoon; a bowline or round turn and two half hitches should be used to secure the line to a bollard or ring. An alternative solution is to make a slip rope, passing the line through a suitable ring or

slot in the cleat, and leading it back to the yacht. The advantages are that all excess line is removed from the pontoon, the line can be adjusted from the yacht, and it is possible to cast off without going ashore.

If a bollard or mooring ring is being used by other yachts, it is courteous to pass your lines underneath so they can remove their own lines easily.

Round turn and two half hitches

A quick and easy knot for attaching a mooring line to a ring, bollard or post.

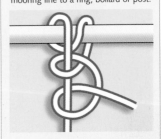

ABOVE **A pre-tied bowline can be used to hold the yacht to its berth while manoeuvring alongside.**

ABOVE **Variations on the conventional cleat provide the simplest solution to mooring.**

GETTING FENDERS IN POSITION ....

1 Fenders are mainly needed to protect the wide part of the yacht. They can be tied to the toerail or guardrail as shown here.

2 A simple overhand knot allows each fender to be untied quickly. Alternatively, use a round turn and two half hitches.

3 Coming alongside all the fenders are out, with the crew holding bow and stern lines and ready to jump onto the dock or pontoon.

Attaching fenders

Fenders are used to protect the side of the yacht. They can be hung from a suitable cleat or from the toerail. They should be concentrated at the wide point of the yacht and any other areas that may be vulnerable. Fenders must hang straight down between the yacht and the pontoon, and be down far enough so they do not ride up and pop out, which can happen when the yacht is pulled in tight to the pontoon and is rocked by the wind or passing traffic. Once underway and free of potential obstructions, the fenders should always be removed and stowed away.

ENTERING A MARINA BERTH ....

1 If there is tide flowing, always come in against the tide to stop the boat.

2 You could either take a pre-tied bowline round the cleat, and allow the skipper to take in the slack.

3 Or use the tail-end of the stern line as a spring led forward to the bow.

4 Adjust the bow and stern line to approximate equal lengths.

Entering a marina berth

A yacht should come alongside a pontoon as slowly as possible, with all fenders in position. Crew must be ready at the bow and stern, holding bow and stern lines. Each line should be secured to the yacht, led through the relevant fairlead, and taken under the lifelines and back to the crew's hand, where it is held in a coil ready to take ashore.

It's normal to go in bows first, with the bow hand jumping ashore just before the bow touches. Don't be over hasty and do this too early. You may fall into the water and risk getting crushed between the yacht and pontoon. Other crew should stand by to fend off if necessary.

As soon as the bow hand drops on the pontoon he or she should run ahead to the next cleat, ring or bollard, and take a turn to stop or "snub" the line and hold the yacht, which should by now have gone into reverse gear in order to take forward way off. This enables the stern hand to jump ashore and take a turn round a cleat, ring or bollard further astern, and by sweating on both lines the yacht can be pulled in close alongside the pontoon. The crew finally makes fast, attaches springs and checks fenders while the skipper closes down the engine.

Leaving a marina berth

Before leaving the skipper checks wind and tide, assesses the proximity of nearby yachts and their rigging, decides on the most practical route from the berth, briefs the crew, informs neighbouring yachts the boat is about to leave and starts the engine.

In straightforward situations the springs will be let off first; in some instances the skipper may need to motor ahead or astern against the pull of a spring, in order to move the stern or bows away from the pontoon. One crew takes responsibility for the bow line and one for the stern line. Either may need to stay on the pontoon with their line snubbed (one turn round the cleat, ring or bollard to hold the yacht) in order to help push out the yacht. They step on board at the last moment, pushing off with the back foot. All crew should be ready to fend off other yachts if necessary. It's better to use a foot than a hand, but never let any part of your body get between boat and boat or boat

and pontoon in case they come hard together. Best of all, dangle a hand-held fender to hold boats apart.

Once clear of the pontoon and marina, the crew should coil and stow all warps and fenders, ensuring they do not obstruct the helmsperson's view while moving around the boat.

SWINGING MOORINGS

These are common in rivers and estuary harbours. A large rubber inflatable buoy is made fast to a ground anchor by chain. The yacht is either secured to a permanent strop attached to the buoy with an eye that slips over the main foredeck cleat or, on a temporary mooring, may use a slip rope through an eye or ring. Smaller mooring buoys are often lifted onto the foredeck, with the strop and chain running out through the anchor fairlead. The mooring should allow the yacht enough room to swing on wind or tide without fouling adjacent moored yachts. It will also rise and fall with the tide.

Permanent deep-water moorings are at a premium in tidal areas where moorings that dry out restrict times for access and sailing.

ABOVE **A boathook is often required to grab a mooring. The skipper must aim to stop the boat dead in the water for a few seconds while the crew gets the mooring line on board.**

REVERSING OUT FROM A MARINA BERTH

1 Depending on wind, tide and neighbouring yachts, you may need to reverse rather than go forward from a berth.

2 The crew lets off the bow line, which is then taken aboard.

3 With the stern line also removed, he holds the yacht on the forward spring.

4 Hauling in the spring pulls the bows into the pontoon and lets the stern blow out.

5 The skipper motors astern as the crew jumps on and pushes off with his back foot.

Leaving a swinging mooring

Before leaving the skipper checks wind and tide, assesses the closeness of nearby yachts, decides on the most practical route from the berth and briefs the crew. If the yacht is lying downwind from the mooring and there are no yachts close by, it makes sense to hoist the mainsail and prepare the headsail before leaving. An experienced skipper may opt to sail off the mooring with the headsail hoisted and backed to help the bow bear off, but if there is any doubt it is wiser to start the engine and motor off.

In most cases the bow hand will lift the mooring strop off the main cleat, and ensure it runs out cleanly through the fairlead when the skipper gives the word and will then shout, "Gone!" The skipper can then let the yacht fall back on the wind or tide, allowing the bow to fall off to one side before moving ahead without danger of running down the mooring – it is exceptionally embarassing to get the mooring line caught round the keel or rudder, and even worse if it is tangled round the prop.

Picking up a swinging mooring

Before approaching the mooring the headsail should be dropped and stowed. Manoeuvring may be considerably easier if the mainsail is also dropped and furled. The approach should always be made uptide or upwind, whichever will stop the yacht.

The skipper should aim to nudge the mooring buoy with one side of the bow, and the yacht must stop moving forwards as soon as it touches. This will enable the bow hand to grab the mooring strop, using a boathook if required, and pull it up through the anchor fairlead and onto the foredeck cleat. Getting this right requires experience and excellent timing. If the bow hand grabs the mooring buoy when it is too far off or too far astern, or the yacht is still moving forwards, starting to move backwards or blowing away from the mooring, he or she will risk being pulled in. In these circumstances it is better to let go of the buoy or strop immediately, and tell the skipper to try again, which will often require a complete 360 degree circuit.

ABOVE **There must always be sufficient room for yachts and other craft to swing on wind and tide when on a mooring. Yachts of different size and motor boats will tend to have different swing characteristics.**

Manoeuvring under power

Great care must be taken when manoeuvring under power in a confined space. A yacht is prone to being blown around by the wind, and will naturally adopt a beam-on position with the bow tending to blow offwind. Yachts react slowly to changes on the tiller or wheel, and may require a strong burst of power to turn upwind. Their steering is also affected by the propeller throwing the stern to one side – if the propeller rotation is clockwise, the stern will move to starboard.

Reversing a yacht can be particularly difficult. The effect of the rudder is limited, windage on the yacht will encourage the bows to blow

ABOVE **When motoring astern, the skipper should be able to face aft. Always keep rudder movements small when going in this direction.**

downwind, and if the helmsperson attempts to turn too fast and too tight the yacht will get locked into a tight groove and continue turning until the stern points directly into the wind.

Always try to manoeuvre and come alongside as slowly as possible, and remember that the heavier the yacht the more effort will be needed to stop it moving forwards. If there is tide running you should endeavour to come alongside facing uptide so the yacht is easy to stop; if there is no tide, choose the upwind direction. You should never need to use more than a small amount of reverse throttle to stop.

ABOVE **The skipper must have a clear view forward when motoring ahead.**

NON TIDAL BERTHING

Sailing areas like lakes, with negligible tidal flow, makes berthing a simple operation.

Bows-on

Mooring bows-on to a quay works well in non tidal areas. The yacht is held to the quay by two bow lines at an angle of about 30 degrees to each other, with a stern line holding it back off the quay. This stern line may be a fixed mooring line, which is picked up from a small floating buoy, or the yacht may have to lay out a stern anchor as it approaches the quay. Care must be taken to ensure fenders protect the boat from yachts on either side, and that spreaders and shrouds will not tangle in a rising wind. A breast line may be necessary to hold the sterns of bows-on yachts together, with each outside yacht running a long line at an acute angle from stern to quay to help prevent the group of yachts from blowing sideways.

Stern-on

Mooring stern-on to a quay uses the same techniques as bows-on. It is easier and more pleasant to hop from stern to quay, particularly if you have a gangway ladder, and to run an anchor from the bows, a larger anchor giving better holding. It is also easier to leave the berth. However, anyone walking along the quay can see the innards of your yacht, which can be a disadvantage. But the principal problem associated with mooring stern-on is that you need to be extremely confident in your ability to reverse.

Rafting

In some cases pressure of space may require yachts to raft-up when moored side-on to a quay or harbour wall. An obvious requirement is that the rafted yachts should become progressively smaller. Springs should be set between each yacht, and long lines taken ashore from the bows and stern of the outside yacht to prevent the raft bending in a downwind direction.

Leaving a raft can be tricky if you are on the inside. The best solution is to wait for everyone else to go. The second best is to tell them your plans, apologize for the inconvenience, and ensure that the new inside yacht has a stern line made up and ready to pull in, with a bow line led round the back of

ABOVE **A raft of boats can lead to all kinds of problems with bending in the middle. It's just as well that this is a light hearted, lunchtime raft in fine weather.**

your yacht. You can then move out forwards with your crew physically holding the raft close alongside, and once your stern clears, the raft's new bow line can be hauled in smartly.

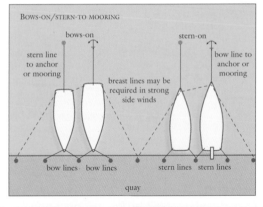

BOWS-ON/STERN-TO MOORING

bows-on

stern line to anchor or mooring

breast lines may be required in strong side winds

bow lines · bow lines

stern-on

bow line to anchor or mooring

stern lines · stern lines

quay

LEFT AND BELOW

In the Mediterranean it is often customary to berth bows-on to a quay, with a mooring or anchor line pulling the stern and holding the bows off. It is not suitable for those who find clambering between pulpit and quay difficult, but it ensures privacy and also saves having to reverse under power.

LEFT Mooring stern-on is de rigeur at floating boat shows where the manufacturers want to welcome potential customers on board, and is also popular in ports such as San Tropez where being seen is all that matters.

Drying out

Against a wall If you are lying alongside a fixed wall with a tidal rise and fall, lines will need to be shortened as the boat comes up and lengthened as it goes down – it is incredibly embarassing and not a little perplexing to return and find your yacht suspended in mid-air.

ABOVE **Drying out enables a full inspection of the bottom of the yacht, without the considerable cost of a boatyard lift. Note the rope from the quay to the mast, which prevents the yacht being lifted outwards by the tide.**

If the tidal fall is so great that your yacht will touch the bottom and dry out, it is reassuring to know that it won't fall over. A bilge keeler will obviously present few problems, while a fin keeler on the other hand will require care and consideration proportional to the length and shape of its keel. The yacht must be leaning slightly inwards to be safe, but not so far as to risk damaging the shrouds. There must be plenty of fendering along the side and, in addition to the standard bow and stern lines and springs, a safety line should be led down from the quay and across the coachroof to the midships outside toerail.

On a mooring or anchorage Bilge keel or lifting keel yachts can dry out safely on a soft bottom such as sand or mud. A fin keel yacht, which dries out with no support, will lie on its side, and everything that is loose will slide around down below causing possible damage to the side or keel of the yacht.

ABOVE **With its daggerboard lifted, the F-24 trimaran can anchor in knee deep water and will dry out virtually level on a sand or mud bottom.**

ANCHORING

A safe anchorage should be well sheltered from prevailing wind and waves, and well away from a lee shore or rocks.

The bottom must have good holding for the anchor. Avoid areas with rocky outcrops, or underwater detritus such as old mooring chains, which may snag and trap your anchor.

There should be sufficient water under the keel at all states of the tide, but it must always be shallow enough for the anchor to hold properly. The length of the anchor chain should be no less than five times the depth of the water; if the anchor is held by a line, its length should be at least seven times the depth of the water.

Choose a spot that will allow you to anchor without fouling chains or lines from other yachts and boats, and with plenty of room to swing freely.

An anchor light should show the position of the yacht at night.

Take some bearings on landmarks to gauge if the anchor starts dragging.

If the wind changes and the holding deteriorates, be prepared to leave the anchorage and seek better protection with minimum delay.

Dropping the anchor

Drop and stow the sails, choose your spot, and slowly motor ahead. The foredeck crew should lay the anchor in the bow fairlead, and ensure the chain or anchor warp is clear for dropping.

ABOVE **A well sheltered anchorage in the Greek islands provides a delightful location for the afternoon, but may become less secure by night with the possibility of a change in the wind direction or strong gusts blowing down the hillside as the temperature falls.**

Engage neutral, and when the yacht stops moving forwards tell the foredeck crew to "Drop the hook!" while engaging reverse. The crew of a small yacht should be able to pay out the warp or chain hand over hand in shallow water. On a larger yacht, or in deeper water, the chain should be let go with the warp securely cleated or held round a windlass to ensure the right amount is paid out. Beware that a fast moving chain is potentially dangerous. Never attempt to stop it with your hands.

As the yacht moves backwards, the chain or warp will be spread along the bottom. Once a sufficient length has been dropped, the helmsperson can reverse a little harder with the chain or warp secured to its cleat or windlass to dig the anchor in. You can then line up two static objects to check it is not dragging.

RIGHT **Multiplying the depth of water below the yacht by a factor of five gives an approximate guide to the right length of chain for a safe holding. A water depth of 5m (16½ft) for instance will require a chain length of 25m (82ft).**

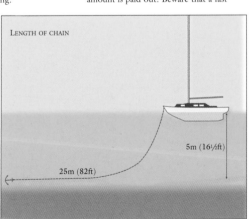

LENGTH OF CHAIN

5m (16½ft)

25m (82ft)

ABOVE **In the ready to anchor position, the anchor shaft should fit snugly in the bow roller fairlead, and be securely locked so it does not fall at an inopportune moment. On most yachts the anchor should never be left in this position while sailing.**

HANDLING THE ANCHOR

Take great care when handling the anchor, which can easily damage the deck or bows.

The chain is also potentially dangerous and prone to bashing the sides of the anchor locker.

It is advisable to wear gloves when handling the chain, and always wear boots or shoes.

Lifting the anchor

The skipper should slowly motor ahead while the foredeck crew pulls up the anchor chain or warp, if it's a chain, he or she may need to use a windlass or crew back-up. Ensure the chain passes cleanly into the anchor locker, and keep the skipper informed of progress. When the chain or warp goes past vertical the skipper should back off to prevent it pulling back and damaging the bows. The crew should be able to feel when the anchor breaks out of the bottom, and tell the skipper who will be prepared for the bow to blow off.

Take great care that the anchor doesn't bash the bows when it comes up to the fairlead. If it's covered in mud or weed, be prepared to dunk it back in the sea for a clean-up or to give it a scrub before stowing. Always wear shoes or boots when handling an anchor.

PULLING UP THE ANCHOR

1 Let the skipper know as soon as the anchor breaks clear of its holding.

2 As you pull in the chain, take care the anchor does not swing back and damage the bow.

3 Brush off weed and dunk the anchor in the sea to remove any mud before you put it away.

4 Ensure the anchor goes in on top of the chain, so everything runs free next time it goes out.

Using a tender

Be very careful when leaving or returning to an anchorage or mooring in a small tender. What should be a pleasant experience can easily turn into a potential nightmare. A few precautions should be followed:

- Do not overload the tender.
- Do not rely solely on a small outboard motor for propulsion. Take oars as well.
- Make sure you know exactly where your yacht is and that you can locate it in the dark.
- Be very wary of strong offshore winds and adverse tides.
- Work out a sensible way of getting to and from the yacht or tender without falling in the sea.
- Wear waterproof clothing and encourage lifejackets all round.
- Don't even think about it if you have drunk too much alcohol.

Sailing manoeuvres

On a yacht, sailing techniques are scaled-up from dinghy practice, with two major differences. First, a heavy keel will provide considerable stability. Second, mechanical aids such as winches must be used to cope with heavier loadings.

SAILING UPWIND

While most dinghies are designed to be sailed virtually flat, keelboats will heel to leeward when sailing upwind in anything more than a light wind. Old-fashioned designs with slim, narrow hulls such as the Dragon 5.5 or 30 Square Metre were designed to heel right over at around 30 degrees or more when beating to windward, increasing their waterline length but giving a very wet ride. Modern designs are much wider and designed to sit upright, but may naturally heel to an angle past 10 degrees. The downward force of gravity provided by the weight of the keel – and to a lesser extent the weight of the crew if they sit up on the windward side – will combine with the upward force of buoyancy in the hull to prevent the yacht heeling further.

In strong or gusty winds a yacht may be knocked down, with water breaking over the leeward deck and running along the sides of the cockpit coamings. This is

perfectly safe and not a cause for panic, as there is too much resistance for the yacht to heel any further. However, it is also a highly ineffective way for a yacht to make ground to windward. Apart from being uncomfortable, with the crew clinging to

the windward side and anything loose getting thrown around down below, the yacht will rapidly lose ground to leeward as it slides on its side while the helm battles with the weather helm caused by a rudder that is half lifted out of the water.

ABOVE **Sailing on a close reach with the wind forward of the beam, the mainsail and genoa are eased and the boat at a comfortable angle of heel.**

ABOVE **When sailing hard on the wind the angle of heel increases, with the crew sitting on the deck to help increase windward leverage. If the wind increases, these yachts would need to shorten sail to maintain the same angle of heel rather than lose speed and slip sideways.**

LEFT **On this racing yacht the sails are sheeted hard in with a virtually perfect slot between genoa and mainsail. All the crew stay up to windward, with the exception of one crew who trims the genoa in and out in response to gusts and lulls.**

ABOVE **The crew needs to ease the mainsheet to break the effect of the slot and depower the rig, allowing the skipper to maintain the same course during a gust or bear away if required.**

If a yacht consistently heels too far, the crew should immediately shorten sail, while ensuring the mainsail and headsail remain balanced and the yacht has neutral helm (rudder not pulling hard in any direction). If the mainsail is too small and the headsail too large, the yacht will develop lee helm and want to bear away; if the mainsail is too large and the headsail too small, the yacht will develop weather helm and want to head up.

When a yacht is knocked down by a gust, the crew should react promptly. The helmsperson should let the yacht follow its natural inclination, which is to luff into the wind. This will help gain ground to windward, as well as bringing the yacht back upright by decreasing pressure on the sails, lifting the front of the mainsail and reducing the slot effect. Once the gust has passed the headsail will back with its windward telltales lifting, and the helm must bear away onto the old course to keep the yacht moving forwards at maximum speed. This is particularly important when

sailing upwind through waves, when the yacht should be sailed free and fast and pitching reduced to a minimum by concentrating crew weight in the middle of the boat.

When sailing on a fetch or close reach, the effects of a temporary knock-down can be reduced by easing off the mainsheet. This may be practical on a very small cruiser when the mainsheet can effectively be hand held, but will require too much

time and physical effort on a larger yacht. It is also uncomfortable and unsettling if done repeatedly, since the mainsheet and boom will tend to flog from side to side.

If the yacht has a traveller, the mainsail can be eased off the centreline to allow the yacht to stay upright during gusts without easing the mainsheet. However, if easing the traveller and letting off the mainsheet fail to keep the yacht upright, the crew must shorten sail.

ABOVE **Sailing upwind on this cruising yacht is altogether a more leisurely affair. An easily handled amount of sail area for the prevailing conditions guarantees maximum comfort for those on board.**

ABOVE **Sailing hard on the wind, the genoa should be wound in until the leech is almost kissing the spreaders. The crew positions here provide maximum power for sheeting in.**

SHEETING SAILS

The primary winches used to control headsails sheets and the multi-purchase systems for mainsheets are extremely powerful, and care must be taken not to oversheet the sails on an upwind course, which will break up the airflow and slow the boat down.

Headsail sheets

The leech of the headsail should be sheeted tight enough for the sail to be close to the end of the leeward spreader, without actually touching it. For optimum performance the crew must watch the headsail as the apparent wind changes, as when accelerating out of a tack.

As the wind increases the sail will stretch away from the leeward spreader, and needs to be sheeted in until it is once again close but not touching. If the wind or boat speed drops the sheet must be eased to pull the sail off the spreaders, while the helmsperson bears away to keep the boat moving.

Both the foot and leech should appear similarly taut when the traveller car is in

LEFT Note how all the sails on these racing 48's appear to set identically. Sheeting positions are precisely governed with regimented settings for all wind conditions.

the correct position. Moving the car forwards will loosen the foot and stretch the leech; moving it back will stretch the foot and loosen the leech. Any fluttering on the leech can be controlled by pulling on the leech line. Do not pull the leech line so tight that you completely kill the flutter as this will effectively hook the sail and spoil the airflow.

Mainsheet

The mainsail should be sheeted in to match the set of the headsail, and never pulled in so tight that it is oversheeted creating a hooked leech that will kill boat speed. Sheet in the mainsail until it just starts to get backwinded by the jib. The front part of both headsail and mainsail will often backwind at the same time.

ABOVE The leech and foot of the genoa should have a similar amount of curve as shown here. If the genoa is reduced by the rolling, the sheet lead must be moved forward.

ABOVE The headsail car has been moved almost to the front of the track on these First Class 8 racers, allowing their jibs to set perfectly.

Safety first

"One hand for the boat!" is a basic law of seamanship which should be understood by both helm and crew. It is particularly important in difficult conditions when the yacht may be heeling, pitching or rolling from side to side. The most obvious application is for the crew who should use their harness safety lines as a failsafe third hand when both other hands are being used to move along the deck or pull in sails.

It is equally important for the helmsperson, as the following true story illustrates. The helmsman of an 8m (26ft) cruising trimaran was sitting on the side deck for a good view forwards, while entering the Needles Channel on a downwind course for the safety of the Solent. This is an area with a reputation for pushing up confused seas created by strong winds and fast tides, and when a rogue wave caught the yacht

ABOVE It is acceptable to stand for a better view while helming, but the maxim "one hand for the boat" should always be adhered to if there is a sea running.

on its windward quarter it was spun round into the wind and heeled over. In ordinary circumstances the helmsman would have hauled in on the tiller to correct the turn. However with nothing to hang onto he fell forwards into the cockpit, inadvertently pushing the tiller hard away so the boat jack-knifed side-on to the wind and was capsized.

ABOVE **A full size geared wheel makes it possible to steer the boat from windward or leeward positions, with the latter (shown here) providing a clear view of yachts and other obstructions that might otherwise be hidden by the genoa.**

This will be clearly shown by the windward side telltales lifting in the bottom half of both headsail and mainsail, while the leeward telltales and those higher up blow back along the line of the sail.

If the leeward telltales hang down, the helmsperson needs to head up into the wind, or the crew needs to ease the sheets. If the windward telltales lift from top to bottom, the helm needs to bear away from the wind to prevent the boat from stalling, or the crew needs to pull in the sails.

CREW POSITION

Where the crew choose to sit or stand on the deck of a yacht are equally important when considering comfort and performance.

Tiller steering

The best position for a helmsperson steering with a tiller is to sit on the windward side of the cockpit, with feet braced to leeward if necessary, and with a clear view forwards along the windward deck. If the tiller has an extension, the helmsperson may opt to sit up on the windward cockpit coaming or side deck, where the view forward is much better and it is easier to watch the sails. However this position is considerably less secure if the boat heels in a gust.

ABOVE **The Mumm 36 is likely to be about the maximum size for a yacht with tiller steering, which is the preferred choice for a more responsive and dinghy-like feel.**

In either case the helm may need to move down to the leeward side of the cockpit occasionally so that he or she can see what is happening behind the headsail, but this should only be regarded as a temporary position.

Wheel steering

When steering, the helmsperson will often have exclusive use of an after cockpit that provides three possible positions: central, windward, or leeward. In all cases the prime requirement is that the helmsperson maintains a clear view and full control.

In the central position a helmsperson is able to stand and get a reasonable view forward, though this may be somewhat obscured by the mast, and the view to leeward will be completely blanketed by a genoa. The main advantage with this position is that both hands can be used on the wheel for maximum control and big movements, and should therefore always be used when sailing downwind.

In the windward position, the helm can either stand or sit. The position chosen will depend on the design of the cockpit, how the floor is sloped, and how much the boat is heeling. Its effectiveness will also depend on the diameter of the wheel and how easily it comes to hand. Good balance and good gearing is likely to be necessary for single-handed control. It should provide a clear view forward and

ABOVE **Racing upwind, the 14 strong crew of this yacht spread their weight evenly along the windward side between mast and stern away from the foredeck where extra weight would create pitching. The crew should also keep their weight to windward when they are off watch down below.**

to windward, as well as a good view of the sails, which is necessary when sailing with the wind forward of the beam.

In the leeward position, the helm will have to sit with his body braced against the guardrail if the boat is heeling, and as far as ballast is concerned is definitely on the wrong side. He or she will be able to get a view forward through the slot between

ABOVE **Sailing downwind, weight is moved aft over the wide, buoyant stern to prevent the bow being pushed down and ensure maximum effectiveness with the rudder.**

the sails as well as being able to see down to leeward behind the genoa, but the view to windward will be totally obscured.

Crew places

On an upwind course the crew should sit on the windward side of the cockpit once the boat starts heeling. For those who wish to sit up on the side deck, the most comfortable position is racing style, with your back to the centreline and legs hanging over the side of the boat. This is safe so long as you are not manoeuvring near other yachts, when legs and other body parts should be kept inboard. The crew should also concentrate their weight amidships, keeping off the bows or stern where extra weight may promote pitching.

On an offwind course the bow of a yacht will tend to go down as speed increases, and the crew should move aft to help keep the rudder down in the water. The crew should trim the boat to keep it level and the mast upright, particularly when sailing dead downwind.

TACKING

In a cruiser, tacking should be a precise, controlled manoeuvre. It cannot be done instantly, as in a small racing dinghy, and should be viewed as a fluid transition that relies on the cruiser constantly moving and not stalling while changing tacks.

Tacking technique

The helmsperson must ensure the boat is footing fast, by bearing away a touch to build speed if necessary and looking for a flat patch between waves.

The crew are prepared by the call of, "Ready about!" In typical circumstances one crew will take responsibility for the leeward active sheet. He or she will uncleat it or take it out of its self-tailer, and hold the free end until the yacht spins round. The other crew will take responsibility for the new active sheet, which is on the windward side of the boat. He or she will put one turn round the winch, and pull in the sheet until all slack is removed. The helm calls "lee-oh!" (helm's-alee!) and

TACKING FROM STARBOARD TO PORT ....

1 As the skipper puts the tiller over, the first crew lets go the headsail sheet ready for the second crew to pull in.

2 The headsail should be sheeted most of the way in before the tack is completed and the sail has filled with wind on the new side.

3 Ready for the first crew to push the handle into the winch and wind the sail hard-in, fine tuning it to the angle and speed of the wind.

turns the boat into the eye of the wind. The aim is to steer the yacht through the tack, matching the tightness of the turn to the speed and efficiency of the crew. It is a great mistake to just slam the rudder right over, because it will act like a brake. As the bows of the yacht turn through the eye of the wind, the headsail starts to back. This is the sign for the first crew to throw the sheet off the winch and let it run free. The best way to do this is to spin the sheet anti-clockwise and upwards off the top of the winch. The second crew

pulls in the new leeward sheet hand over hand, as much and as fast as possible. As soon as the sheet starts to pull hard, he or she puts a second turn on the winch and can then pull in more sheet until it is necessary to use the handle. At this point a third and possibly a fourth turn can be put on, though beware of riding turns that jam the winch if too many turns ride up. The tail end can then be wrapped round the self-tailing jaws, and the first crew can insert the winch handle and start to wind. Alternatively and more

quickly the second crew can hand hold the sheet end and pull in as the other crew winds.

One person must watch the leech and be ready to stop winding as it closes on the spreader. While this is going on the helm will have turned the yacht onto the new tack, and may need to luff to allow the crew to sheet the sail in faster. He or she can then bear away to build up speed, while the sheet is wound in as the sail stretches away from the spreaders.

TACKING FROM PORT TO STARBOARD ....

1 The leeward crew spins the sheet anti-clockwise off the winch.

2 It is vital that the old active sheet runs free and allows the new sheet to be pulled in.

3 The new sheet is then locked in place into the self-tailing jaws.

4 Allowing one crew to complete sheeting in the sail.

Tacking problems

- The sheets may catch on a cleat or winch around the mast area, which is normally the result of pulling in too slowly. If this happens one crew will need to move smartly forward to lift the sheet off the obstruction.
- If the yacht fails to tack round, it is simply going too slowly and the sheet has been thrown off too soon leaving insufficient power in the headsail to help pull the bows round.
- If the crew have difficulty winding in the sheet on the new tack, they are probably too slow pulling in hand over hand, or the helm may be bearing away too quickly. In most cases the crew should be able to pull virtually all the sheet in hand over hand reserving use of the winch handle for fine tuning.

SAILING OFFWIND

The effect of less apparent wind, coupled with a noticeably warmer airflow, frequently make sailing offwind a real pleasure after the rigours of a hard beat into the wind.

Reaching

When sailing on a beam or broad reach, the headsail should be eased until the windward telltales are just lifting. The mainsheet traveller should be let off to the end of the track, and the mainsheet eased until the mainsail's windward telltales are just lifting. The kicking strap or vang should be pulled hard down. If the yacht heels too far it will start to slip sideways, and the speed of a reaching course will exacerbate the tendency to weather helm with the result that the helm has to strain to hold the tiller or wheel. The solution is to shorten sail or bear away further downwind to reduce side-on sail pressure.

Running

On a downwind course the mainsheet should be sheeted in enough to hold the sail off the shrouds and spreaders, which will damage the coating on the sail and leave an unsightly dark mark over a period of time.

ABOVE **Holding out the headsail with the boat hook may be OK in very light winds, but is not recommended when sailing downwind.**

LEFT **Fast and furious. The gennaker (left) and spinnaker (right) give tremendous power when sailing downwind on a reach, and are recommended for those who enjoy knife edge thrills in this kind of close quarters situation.**

On a dead downwind course a standard headsail will be blanketed by the mainsail. It will be considerably more effective if it is goose-winged (wing on wing) to windward, but will require some kind of pole to hold it out. A genoa may be too large and low to be flown effectively, even when used with a topping lift to hold the pole clear of the water. If the pole end persists in catching, probably the best solution is to change to a smaller headsail.

Sailing under mainsail alone, a yacht will tend to luff to windward. A goose-winged cruising chute or spinnaker will help keep the yacht in balance and add to speed.

Spinnakers

For cruisers, spinnaker principles are as on dinghies, except that everything is scaled up with larger poles that require topping lifts, and downhauls, and sheet and guy controlled by the primary winches.

Rolling downwind

If there are waves, a yacht will be prone to roll downwind. A wave that hits on the windward quarter (side of the stern) will make the yacht luff and heel to windward, while a wave hitting the leeward quarter will make it bear away and heel to leeward. The pendulum effect of the keel can rapidly build up a rolling motion. This motion will be exacerbated by natural imbalance in the sails. On a beat or reach the sideways force in the sails will press the rig down and prevent the boat rolling. On a run the wind is directly behind, and the force in the sails will tend to see-saw from side to side. A primary control is to ensure the kicking strap is pulled tight, reducing twist in the top of the sail, which would otherwise encourage the yacht to heel to windward.

A rudder is relatively ineffectual while the stern is being driven to one side or the other by a wave. Course

ABOVE **The effect of waves lifting the stern with the mainsail to one side and the spinnaker to the other will promote rolling, which can only be controlled by good sailing technique.**

corrections must be anticipated, and made before a wave hits and while the yacht is sailing in a trough or flat patch where rudder movements will have maximum effect. If a yacht is travelling fast in strong winds, the crew should move aft and stay off the foredeck when possible. It is vital to keep all of the rudder down in the water for maximum steerage.

To achieve perfect balance, a yacht sailing downwind with a spinnaker should be heeled slightly to windward to offset the push of the mainsail, with the centreline of the spinnaker (from head to halfway between tack and clew) vertical and the foot horizontal, which means having tack and clew at exactly the same height. The spinnaker pole should be pulled back at right angles to the apparent wind, with the inboard end of the pole raised so it is at right angles to the mast. In reality the crew can only attempt to get close to this level of perfection, and the spinnaker will always pull to one side or the other.

Letting the spinnaker blow forwards will drive the bows down and promote instability and rolling. To prevent this, the clew and tack of a spinnaker should be pulled down as low as possible to flatten the sail and bring its centre of effort aft, with both corners at exactly the same height. Sheet in the spinnaker to help the yacht luff up, and sheet out to help it bear away.

ABOVE **The uphaul and downhaul control the vertical angle of the spinnaker pole and ensure that clew and tack are virtually level.**

Cruising chutes

A cruising chute is a safer, simpler option for downwind cruising. It lacks the ultimate power of a spinnaker, but is much easier for short-handed or inexperienced crew to use. Cruising chutes are variations on dinghy gennakers, cut with an asymmetric tack and clew and using port and starboard sheets. Flat-cut chutes can be carried close to the wind on a broad or beam reach.

Coiling a line

Unused lines and the ends of lines should always be coiled so that they are neat and tidy, and will run out in the case of a sheet or halyard, or can be thrown in the case of a mooring line.

- Always coil rope clockwise, turning each loop through a half turn to avoid forming figure of eights. This is much easier with a soft rope.
- To secure the coil, take two or more turns round the top part of the coil. Then pass the free end through as a loop, which can be locked off against the coil. This will enable the coil to be hung from a winch or cleat.

BELOW **A perfectly balanced spinnaker would have an imaginary vertical line from the head to the halfway point of the foot, and an imaginary horizontal line between clew and tack.**

ABOVE **The Japanese racer could bear away to correct the roll to windward, but will risk sailing into the wind shadow of the chasing USA boat. Trimming in the guy and letting out the sheet would also help pull the yacht upright.**

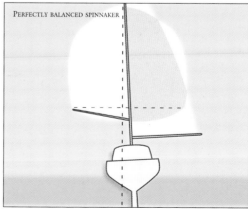

PERFECTLY BALANCED SPINNAKER

Full-cut chutes are more effective down-wind, but may require a pole to goose-wing on the opposite side to the mainsail.

The tack of the chute is attached to the yacht by a variable length strop that is led into the pulpit in front of the forestay. The strop adjusts leech tension and clew height: tight and short for reaching and loose and long for running. If rolling is a problem, the strop of the chute should be shortened to bring the sail aft and the sheet should be taken in.

Sheet in the chute to help the yacht luff up, and sheet out to help it bear away.

Using a dousing sock

A standard method of launching a cruising chute is to use a dousing sock. The chute is hoisted inside its dousing sock, with the crew taking care to keep the halyard and sock clear of the spreaders and forestay. Once the halyard is fully up and made fast, the dousing sock is pulled to the top of the sail. This lets the sail blow free, and it should be smartly sheeted in to prevent it wrapping round the forestay.

As in a dinghy it is easiest to hoist and set the chute on a downwind course, using the blanketing effect of the mainsail to prevent the sail from blowing out of control. The blanketing effect should also be used when dousing and dropping the chute. The sheet must be freed off to

ABOVE **Nowhere to go. This yacht needs to bear away to avoid an imminent broach, but is held upwind by the boat to leeward.**

allow the dousing sock to be pulled back down over the sail, after which it can be dropped and fed into its bag like a sausage.

GYBING

Cruiser gybes are not as fast or furious as a dinghy, but the power of the mainsail can be awesome when the boom crosses from side to side, and the gybe must be controlled at all times.

Gybing technique

Warn the crew with a, "Ready to Gybe!", and ensure everyone is well clear of the path of the boom, it is vital that no one

pops their head out of the companionway at the critical moment when the boom comes across.

The crew must ensure that there is nothing to prevent the boom from gybing and that the kicking strap is tensioned to hold the boom down. The helmsperson or crew should centralize the mainsheet traveller ready for the gybe, so the traveller car doesn't whistle from side to side with the possibility of smashing itself on the buffers.

The helm cries, "Gybe-oh!" as he or she steers into the gybe. Once the yacht enters the dead downwind zone, helm or crew should haul in the mainsheet, taking in as much as possible so the whole lot cannot crash from side to side. The helmsperson or crew may help the boom across by handing the falls of the main-sheet, which must immediately be paid out hand over hand on the new gybe. At the same time the crew must gybe the head-sail, cruising chute or spinnaker, using much the same techniques as for a dinghy.

As the yacht gybes it may have a tendency to pivot on its keel and turn up into the wind. The helm should counter this by applying rudder correction and bearing away immediately after the gybe, in order to keep the yacht heading downwind.

Gybing problems

It pays to wait for a lull to gybe, but as with a dinghy the effects of apparent wind will be minimized if the boat is sailing fast.

Broaching

This is to be avoided. It is a phenomenon in which a yacht sailing on a downwind course suddenly pivots into the wind, resulting in a total loss of control and lying on its side with most of the rudder lifted clear of the water. It causes particular problems when flying a spinnaker, as the wind will continue to blow up from the foot to the head of the spinnaker, keeping the top of the sail full and holding the yacht down on its side. Releasing the guy is the only way to depower the spinnaker and bring the boat back upright.

ABOVE **Releasing the sheet and letting the spinnaker flog is one way to bring the boat back up, but when sailing this close to the wind the solution is to drop it.**

GYBING FROM STARBOARD TO PORT ....

1 One of the crew begins pulling in the mainsheet while the other stands by to let go of the headsail sheet.

2 When the mainsail comes over the boom should be sheeted right in to reduce the effect of the boom crashing across to the new side.

3 Then the mainsheet is paid out and the headsail trimmed in until both sails are correctly set up for the wind direction on the new gybe.

Do not pull the mainsheet in too early when going into the gybe as this will increase the yacht's tendency to luff and possibly broach. Avoid a situation where the boom hits the new leeward shroud with a thud. Do not head up on to a new reaching course until the boom is let right out, or the boat will heel over, develop weather helm and round up further than you aimed.

Involuntary gybes

On a full downwind course there is the danger of an involuntary gybe, which must be taken seriously when the force of the boom could sweep crew over the side and cause severe injury. In fact a small number of people have lost their lives in this way.

It is vital to keep the boom pulled hard down with the kicking strap, which can be led to the toerail and used as a preventer. This will help prevent the boom starting to move through the first stages of an involuntary gybe, but should never be totally relied on. If the wind is strong and a yacht is sailing well by the lee – usually due to an uncontrolled roll to windward – the force of wind hitting the wrong side of the sail may tear the preventer out of its mounting and the speed with which the boom crashes over will be even more violent.

ABOVE **A relatively flat-cut cruising chute can be comfortably carried on an apparent wind beam reach and will behave much the same as a dinghy gennaker.**

Cruising

Life in the confined space of a yacht can be extremely pleasureable so long as a few common sense rules are adhered to. Tidiness, hygiene and consideration towards other crew members are important, particularly in less than perfect conditions.

Living on board
Take as little baggage as possible. Only use soft bags that can be shoved into cramped spaces. Stow your gear carefully and tidily, so you can find it when you need it at all times. Be considerate to the gear of other crew members. Take great care not to spread water around when changing out of wet gear. Stow waterpoofs and boots where they can drain and dry.

Choose a berth for the duration of your time on board. Pilot berths, which are outboard of the main saloon area, and quarter berths in the aft quarters may have the advantage of being out of the way if you want to lie down during the day. Berths in the forepeak are likely to be uncomfortable when the yacht is sailing.

If a sailing trip requires alternating watches (such as 4 hours on, 4 hours off), respect the rights of those coming off watch and be prepared to take their places immediately on your turn.

Cooking
One crew person may volunteer to do all the cooking. In other cases cooking should be done on a rota, as should washing-up and clearing-up.

ABOVE **Modern yacht galleys can be extremely luxurious and come complete with features such as pressurized hot and cold water. However it is important that the galley also functions in a seaway with a stove mounted on gimbals, secure storage and everything to hand.**

ABOVE **All the delights of cruising life with lunch served up on the front door.**

LEFT The crew down on the leeward deck isn't being sick, though he could well be. Seasickness effects many yachtsmen and is nothing to be ashamed of.

Learn to cook using gimbals and a bum strap, with fiddles to hold pots or kettles in position. The galley should be well ventilated when cooking under way. A stuffy atmosphere with the gas lit can soon lead to nausea. It is also a good idea to wear bib overalls and sea boots while cooking when under way to guard against substances such as boiling water. You should stick to food that is quick and simple to prepare, and food that can be consumed without danger of burns or spillage when under way. Variations on

ABOVE **First aid and basic medical care for those on the boat are vital accessories for enjoyable cruiser sailing.**

hot drinks and soups in half-filled mugs will suffice if all else fails. The galley is best kept clean and tidy at all times, with everything stowed in case the yacht rolls or heels too far.

If you have the luxury of pressurized water, use the power sparingly, and never throw your garbage over the side.

Seasickness

This is a complaint that many suffer from due to an imbalance of the inner ear and is nothing to be ashamed of. Furthermore, although you may feel nauseous for a time, you will normally get over it. If you are not able to take your mind off feeling sick by keeping busy, the best remedy is to get your head down, by getting into your berth and wrapping up and keeping warm in a sleeping bag. You should eat simple food, such as plain bread, and keep drinking to avoid dehydration. There are many remedies commercially available for seasickness, find one that works for you.

If you are sick, take care where you do it. The lavatory is not a very nice place to be. Throwing up over the side, always to leeward, requires care if you are not to fall over. A bucket in the cockpit may be the most acceptable solution, and it is surprising how sympathetic other crew members will be.

Personal hygiene

Keeping good hygiene standards is always important. Familiarize yourself with your marine toilet, and the workings of the sea cocks, which allow water to be pumped in and out. The lavatory can be a nauseous place in rough weather, so make sure you always leave it well pumped and clean, and ensure maximum ventilation. A few countries require yachts to have holding tanks, which are pumped out in marinas. Hopefully the rest of the world will eventually follow suit.

ABOVE **Soggy, wet and cold, the lavatory can be a ghastly place when out at sea. Good ventilation and high standards of cleanliness are essential.**

Emergency action

Most yachtsmen spend a lifetime afloat without ever needing to put any emergency procedures into practice. But if the worst should happen, it pays to be prepared and to have a clear idea of what action is likely to be the most effective.

HEAVING-TO

This technique can be used to bring a yacht to a virtual stop, with almost no forward movement and minimal leeway depending on the strength of the wind.

Heaving-to is associated with riding out a storm, and can be used when conditions are too uncomfortable to sail upwind and there is sufficient open sea to leeward. It can also be used to stall a yacht in any conditions – to make repairs, reef the sails or allow another yacht to catch up.

The basic technique of heaving-to is to sheet the headsail (or storm jib if riding out a gale) to windward so that it is backwinded, free the mainsheet (with the mainsail reefed right down and sheeted in for a gale), and lash the tiller to leeward or the wheel hard down to windward. The opposing forces of rudder and backwinded headsail should hold the yacht in the hove-to position, though it may be necessary to adjust rudder, sheet or sail size to ensure the boat is perfectly balanced, side-on and drifting slowly downwind.

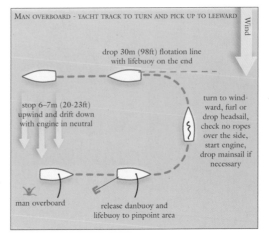

MAN OVERBOARD - YACHT TRACK TO TURN AND PICK UP TO LEEWARD

Wind

drop 30m (98ft) flotation line with lifebuoy on the end

stop 6–7m (20-23ft) upwind and drift down with engine in neutral

turn to windward, furl or drop headsail, check no ropes over the side, start engine, drop mainsail if necessary

man overboard

release danbuoy and lifebuoy to pinpoint area

LEFT Man overboard procedure will depend on a variety of factors. This example presumes a simple situation in which the yacht can release a buoy, turn to windward, drop sails and motor back upwind of the casualty. Wind, waves, tidal flow and darkness may all make the procedure considerably more difficult.

MAN OVERBOARD

Falling overboard is a rare occurrence that strikes in the most unlikely circumstances. Contrary to popular belief it does not always happen in strong winds and survival conditions, mostly because the crew will invariably be clipped on by a safety line. Nor is it reserved for inexperienced sailors.

Falling overboard can happen to anyone any time – getting knocked over by the boom, losing your footing while moving along the deck or when attempting to get into a dinghy.

It is generally easiest to pick up the person overboard from the leeward side, though beware of the yacht being driven over him or her in strong winds or waves. Picking up to windward removes this problem, but the yacht will be prone to blow away from the person overboard and it may be impossible for him or her to climb up or be pulled up on the high windward side. A member of the crew should have the boat hook ready to catch on to the lifejacket or harness of the person being rescued.

MAN OVERBOARD – GOOD PRACTICE

1 Get your crew to practise retrieving a man overboard with a fender.

2 One crewman must keep watching the "casualty".

3 Do not run over the "casualty" – approach with dropped sails.

4 Work out how you will get the "casualty" on board.

Man overboard technique

Make a habit of practising man overboard technique on a regular basis. The standard procedures are as follows:

- Yell, "Man overboard!" as soon as it happens.
- Throw the pushpit-mounted lifebelt over the back of the boat and let the line run out.
- Get someone to watch the person in the water as it is very easy to lose sight if there are waves.
- Take a compass bearing in order to be able to head back along the reciprocal (reverse) course. Start the engine.
- If the person overboard is close enough, the skipper may be able to turn into wind or heave-to without losing ground while the person in the water grabs the lifebelt and line.
- The yacht may need to tack or gybe round, whichever is quickest and most practical, to back-track for the retrieval. Keep the arc of the turn as tight as possible, and ensure the yacht does not drop too far to leeward during a gybe.
- The skipper should aim to bring the yacht to a standstill alongside the person overboard, ideally heaving-to.

Getting back on board

It can be extremely difficult to get someone back on board, particularly when he or she is unable to assist through exhaustion, shock and hypothermia, and the crew must ensure they do not fall over as well. If the crew cannot physically haul a person in over the toerail, it may be possible to use one of the following methods:

- Drop a boarding ladder over the side, or provide a knotted rope for the person in the water to hold onto.
- Launch the yacht's inflatable tender, and roll the person into it.
- Get the person round to the stern, and use the fixed boarding ladder.
- Use the main boom as a derrick supported by the topping lift, and haul the person up with the bottom block of the mainsheet attached to the harness. Or use the kicking strap in conjunction with the headsail halyard.

Basic safety equipment

Radar reflector For use when near shipping channels. The reflector must be hoisted as high as possible.

Distress flares Crew should know where they are located, and read the instructions explaining what each type of flare is for and how to operate them. Yachts must have in-date flares, but out-of-date flares can still be carried as back-up. Hand-held flares have a range of up to 3 miles and are most effective during the day. Hand-launched parachute flares can have a range of over 7 miles and are most effective at night.

Fire extinguisher This needs to be sited in the companionway for immediate use in the galley or cockpit.

Lifebelt Horseshoe-shaped lifebelts have replaced the old-fashioned circular lifebuoy. The lifebelt should be securely mounted on the pushpit so it can be removed with a one-handed throw, with a floating line of at least 50m (164ft) running free. The line may be attached to an automatic floating light.

Flashlight A powerful, hand-held flashlight should be to hand with fully charged batteries.

IOR Dan Buoy Offshore racing yachts must be equipped with a fibreglass weighted pole that floats vertically, with a flag and flashing light visible at 1.6km (1mile). This should be thrown to mark the position of a person overboard.

Radio beacons The yacht may be fitted with an emergency radio beacon that will transmit its exact position to land-based rescue organisations via the SARSAT/COSPAS satellite system. In addition crew members may carry personal radio beacons, which send out a distress signal on VHF Channel 16 and other emergency frequencies.

Life raft Most modern life rafts are mounted on the deck in a hard plastic container, with an automatic inflation system, which must be serviced by the supplier regularly. Standard features include full overhead cover plus double floor and buoyancy compartments, water stabilization to prevent capsize and a full inventory of safety and survival equipment.

Electronics and navigation

For many years conventional navigation relied on the use of land bearings with a chart, compass and plotter or parallel rules inshore, and a fiendishly complex sextant offshore. The introduction of increasingly sophisticated electronics changed all that, with early systems such as Decca, Loran and Radar soon replaced by the ubiquitous global positioning system (GPS), now established as the main navigation system for all marine uses.

The emergence of GPS

GPS provides worldwide navigational coverage via 24 Navstar satellites, which were originally launched by the US Ministry of Defense. Following the relaxation of limits imposed for non-military personnel, GPS now guarantees accuracy within a few metres when sailing between specific points, or waypoints, on a chart. It is available at low cost, with a choice of mounted or hand-held receivers that

ABOVE **The Yeoman plotter is a sophisticated instrument that links electronic navigation with the traditional chart.**

ABOVE **The GPS makes navigation seem easy, but a crew must also be able to read a chart and use a conventional plotter to find the way.**

provide immediate graphic information on a yacht's course, plus any error.

The emergence of GPS has also signalled the beginning of the end for traditional two dimensional charts, which are gradually being replaced by electronic digital charts. Electronic charts can provide features such as tidal information, showing the precise depth for a specific time and

date at any location. Multi-language electronic micro charts used with LCD plotters are already widely available for popular yachting areas. They allow the navigator to scroll through the appropriate chart on a screen, zoom in for the required amount of detail, and plot the position for the yacht, which is automatically displayed with the next waypoint, as well as having

Night lights

- A sailing vessel under way must exhibit side lights (green and red) and a stern light (white).
- A sailing vessel of less than 20m (66ft) may carry these lights as one combined lantern at or near the masthead.
- A sailing vessel of less than 7m (23ft) should carry these lights if practicable. If not, a white flashlight must be ready.
- A sailing vessel under power must exhibit an additional white masthead light.
- A sailing vessel of more than 7m (23ft) must show an all-round white light at a mooring or anchorage.

ABOVE **Most modern yachts are fitted with a combination tri-colour light at the top of the mast (top) rather than a separate port, starboard and stern light (bottom).**

ABOVE **Most yachts of medium size and above now boast an impressive array of electronic navigational and go fast equipment with read-outs available for skipper, crew and navigator. It's still a lot of fun to sail by the seat of your pants though.**

immediate access to speed, depth and wind information.

However all cruiser sailors must accept that electronic navigation can fail in a harsh marine environment. It is vital to be able to fall back on conventional techniques, and they can be great fun to use:

- Taking a fix with a hand-held compass.
- Plotting a course or fixing a position on a traditional chart.
- Correcting magnetic deviation, and allowing for leeway and tidal flow.
- Steering by the compass.
- Recording distance covered by the log.

Multi-function electronics

Modern electronic navigation systems provide immediate access to multiple functions, with the main unit normally located in the navigation area and LED displays for the helmsperson and crew in the cockpit. A popular system such as the B&G Hydra 2000 provides a huge amount of data on speed, depth, wind conditions and course, with a choice of three

categories and nine display pages brought up at the press of a button:

Speed/Depth Boatspeed/depth, boatspeed/speed over ground, boatspeed/apparent wind angle.
Wind Apparent wind speed/apparent wind angle, true wind speed/true wind direction, velocity made good/true wind angle.
Navigation Current heading/course over ground, heading/boatspeed, distance to waypoint/bearing to waypoint.

The IALA buoyage system

The system has been established by the International Association of Lighthouse Authorities (IALA) to create a uniform buoyage throughout the world. System A covers Europe while system B covers America, Korea, Japan and the Philippines.

Lateral marks show the way into and out of channels and ports. Starboard-hand marks (which must be left to starboard on the way in) are conical buoys or spar pillars with a cone on top. Port hand

marks are can shaped buoys or spar pillars with a can on top. Under IALA System A, starboard hand buoys are green or black and port hand buoys are red. Under IALA System B these colours are reversed.

Cardinal marks are yellow and black buoys or spar pillars, which show where it is safe to navigate round a hazardous area such as a shallow water. The location of the hazard is indicated by conical pointers: for instance a cardinal mark to the north of the hazard will have two cones pointing upwards, while a cardinal mark to the south of the hazard will have two cones pointing downwards.

Isolated danger marks are sited directly over a specific danger, such as a wreck. They are black and red pillar or spar buoys with two black spheres on top.

Safe water marks, which indicate that there is navigable water all round, are red and white spherical, pillar or spar buoys.

Special marks are used to indicate specific use of an area, such as underwater cables, and are yellow with an X top mark.

Rights of way

Under sail
- Port gives way to starboard.
- Windward yacht keeps clear.
- Overtaking yacht keeps clear.

Power and sail
- Power gives way to sail.
- Sail gives way to power in restricted waters.
- Sail gives way to a fishing vessel using nets, lines or trawls, but not to a pleasure boat using trolling lines.

Under power
- Right is right! Port-side vessel gives way and must avoid crossing ahead.
- When two vessels are head to head, both turn to starboard.
- Overtaking vessel keeps clear.
- Avoid impeding safe passage of a vessel constrained by its draught.
- Keep to the starboard side of a narrow channel or fairway, where vessels of less than 20m (66ft) must give way.

UNDER POWER: RIGHT IS RIGHT

stop or change course: yacht to port must give way and should avoid attempting to cross ahead

yacht on the starboard side has right of way

under power
under power

KEEP TO THE STARBOARD SIDE

under power
under power

To avoid collision both yachts must turn to starboard. If in a channel, vessels must keep to starboard side.

IALA SYSTEM A BUOYS.....................

1 Hazard to the north.

2 Hazard to the south.

3 Navigable water all round.

4 Starboard side of channel (entering).

5 Port side of channel (entering).

Keelboat classes

Open keelboats represent a traditional category, epitomised by the Dragon and a host of local classes, which can be found in yachting centres around the world.

Dragon
First launched 1929
Designer Johan Anker (Denmark).
LOA 8.89m (29ft)
Beam 1.95m (6ft)
Upwind sail area 27.7 sq m (298 sq ft)
Spinnaker 23.6 sq m (254 sq ft)

A beautiful three-person racing keelboat, which was selected for the 1948 Olympics and remained an Olympic class through to the 1972 Games. Classic wooden Dragons still race with gleaming varnished hulls, but many owners opt for lower maintenance fibreglass, which was introduced to the class in 1973. Fleets of this classic thoroughbred are concentrated in Europe and Scandinavia, as well as the USA, Canada, Japan, Hong-Kong, Australia and New Zealand.

Etchells
First launched 1966
Designer Skip Etchells (USA).
LOA 9.3m (31ft)
Beam 2.1m (7ft)
Upwind sail area 28.5 sq m (307 sq ft)
Spinnaker 48 sq m (517 sq ft)

ABOVE **The Etchells lays claim to being the most popular of modern, open keelboats with top class racing worldwide.**

The International Etchells 22 has more than fifty fleets worldwide scattered through Europe, the USA, Canada, Bermuda, Australia, New Zealand and Hong Kong. The boat is known as a fast, stable and sleek one-design that is normally dry-sailed (kept on shore) and can be raced competitively by three or four average ability sailors, although top-class professional helms also sail in the class for relaxation and pleasure.

ABOVE **The Dragon is a distinguished class which harks back to another era. With slim hull and low freeboard it can also give a very wet ride to windward in windy weather.**

LEFT **With more than half a century behind it, the Flying Fifteen is established as a modern classic and the most famous creation of Uffa Fox.**

RIGHT **The 2.4 Metre provides a unique experience in single-handed racing.**

Flying Fifteen

First launched 1947
Designer Uffa Fox (UK)
LOA 6.1m (20ft)
Beam 1.52m (5ft)
Upwind sail area 13.94 sq m (150 sq ft)
Spinnaker 13.94 sq m (150 sq ft)

A classic two-person racing keelboat, which is often raced by mixed crews, and hails from Britain's centre of yachting at Cowes in the Isle of Wight. The class has a strong international following in Australia, New Zealand, Hong Kong, Ireland and South Africa. Over 3,500 boats have been built in the first 50 years and fibreglass has replaced moulded wood as the modern building material.

International Six Metre

First launched 1907
Designer Various
LOA approximately 11m (36ft)
Beam 2m (6½ft)
Upwind sail area approximately 65 sq m (700 sq ft)
Spinnaker 85 sq m (915 sq ft)

A classic formula racing keelboat that might top anyone's list as the most beautiful class on the water. The main features of the Six are long, lean hulls with classic overhangs that find their full expression in older wooden yachts. Modern designs, built in hi-tech plastics keep taking the class forward, giving formidable upwind performance with a 60 degree tacking angle and enough sail area to keep a five strong crew fully occupied. There are fleets in Britain, Germany, Sweden, Norway, Finland, Switzerland, Argentina and the USA.

Soling

First launched 1965
Designer Jan Linge (Norway)
LOA 8.2m (27ft)
Beam 1.9m (6ft)
Upwind sail area 21.7 sq m (233 sq ft)
Spinnaker 8.75m (29ft) max circumference

The Soling took part in its 13th Olympic regatta at Sydney in 2000, and claimed to be the only gender mixed class at the 1996 Games. Its quickness, manoeuvrability and tactical effectiveness make it particularly suitable for smooth water sailing, and enabled the Soling to introduce the concept of match racing to the Olympics. Soling are sailed all over the world, and the largest fleets are found in the USA, Canada, Australia, Japan, South Africa, Argentina, Brazil and throughout Europe.

ABOVE **At Olympic level the Soling is a powerful boat, its fast response making it a perfect choice for boat-on-boat racing.**

RIGHT **There's nothing like the classical beauty of a 6 Metre racing yacht.**

2.4 Metre

First launched 1988
Designers Various
LOA 4.1–4.35m (13–14ft)
Beam 0.75–0.9m (2½–3ft)
Upwind sail area 8 sq m (86 sq ft)

The 2.4 Metre originated from Sweden, and is a miniature sister to 6 Metre, 8 Metre and 12 Metre (America's Cup) class yachts, which are all designed to a measurement formula. The helmsperson sits facing forward, and controls are within easy reach, the rudder moved by foot pedals.

The 2.4 was awarded International status in 1992, with regular World Championships attracting 60–100 boats. It was also selected as the single-handed class for the disabled sailors' Paralympics at Sydney 2000. There are large fleets in Scandinavia, Italy, England and Australia.

In 1991 the Norlin III made its appearance and has been the dominant design ever since. Rule-bending and the use of exotic materials, which could make old designs obsolete, is strongly discouraged, and the class provides a unique form of single-handed match racing.

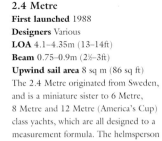

Sportsboat classes

These boats are small, fast, day sailing keelboats, which aim to provide similar thrills to a high performance dinghy, with action packed racing for a crew of five or more. This selection includes half a dozen of the most popular sportsboat classes drawn from around the world, providing excellent competition.

LEFT The Beneteau 25 may be fast and fun, but this crewman appears to be having more than a few problems with the spinnaker.

Beneteau 25
Popular sportsboat produced by Europe's largest yacht builder.
Country of origin France
First launched 1998
Designer Bruce Farr Yacht Design (New Zealand/USA)
LOA 7.5m (25ft)
Beam 2.6m (8½ft)
Displacement 1,250kg (2,755lb)
Upwind sail area 32.5 sq m (350 sq ft)
Spinnaker 48 sq m (517 sq ft) asymmetric
Crew 4–5

BELOW The Hunter 707 provides excellent, dinghy-style racing with its big main and small jib sail plan.

Hunter 707
Top choice sportsboat in Britain, with total one-design specification.
Country of origin UK
First launched 1997
Designer David Thomas (UK)
LOA 7.07m (23ft)
Beam 2.49m (8ft)
Displacement 1,060kg (2,337lb)
Upwind sail area 29.7 sq m (320 sq ft)
Spinnaker 51 sq m (549 sq ft)
Crew 4–5

Bull 7000
A lifting keel sportsboat with cruiser style accommodation for four adults.
Country of origin UK
First launched 1997
Designer Greg Young (New Zealand)
LOA 7.5m (25ft)
Beam 2.45m (8ft)
Displacement 1,100kg (2,425lb)
Upwind sail area 35.1 sq m (378 sq ft)
Gennaker 55 sq m (592 sq ft)
Crew 4–5

ABOVE The Bull 7000 boasts a lifting keel, and gennaker set from a swinging bowsprit, as well as four berths down below.

ABOVE **The Mumm 30 is at the top of the size range for sportsboats.**

ABOVE **The 1720 comes close to the open keelboat concept without cruising accommodation.**

1720

A sportsboat targeted at a wider age and ability range than its rivals.
Country of origin Ireland
First launched 1997
Designer Tony Castro (Ireland)
LOA 8m (26ft)
Beam 2.5m (8ft)
Displacement 1,365 kg (3,009lb)
Upwind sail area 44 sq m (474 sq ft)
Spinnaker 69 sq m (743 sq ft) asymmetric
Crew 455kg (1,003lb) weight limit

Mumm 30

A sportsboat chosen for the Tour de France a la Voile and one-design racing.
Country of origin USA
First launched 1997
Designer Bruce Farr Yacht Design (New Zealand/USA)
LOA 9.43m (30ft)
Beam 3.08m (10ft)
Displacement 2,040 kg (4,497 lb)
Upwind sail area 57 sq m (613 sq ft)
Spinnaker Asymmetric and non asymmetric
Crew 525 kg (1,157 lb) weight limit

Melges 24

The Melges 24 was soon granted full international recognition as the most successful sportsboat worldwide, providing the very top levels of competition.
Country of origin USA
First launched 1996
Designer Reichel/Pugh (USA)
LOA 7.32m (24ft)
Beam 2.5m (8ft)
Displacement 780kg (1,720lb)
Upwind sail area 35.31 sq m (380 sq ft)
Spinnaker 62 sq m (667 sq ft)
Crew 360kg (794lb) weight limit

ABOVE **The Melges 24 can claim to be the most popular and successful sportsboat in the world.**

The world races

Each year sees at least one high profile round-the-world race take place, with a mixture of formats.

The Volvo Ocean Race

Originally known as the Whitbread Round the World Race. This event for fully crewed racing yachts with stop-overs was first held in 1971, when it was a fairly leisurely affair won by a Mexican crew on a stock Swan 65 cruiser-racer. It has been staged every four years since then, and has evolved into a series of full-on sprint stages. The entry was restricted to 18m (59ft) monohulls in 1997 when Paul Cayard (USA) skippered EF Language to victory, after which Volvo took over as main sponsor and renamed the event.

BT Global Challenge

This race was created by Chay Blyth as a 48,279km (30,000 mile) circumnavigation with stop-overs, held the wrong way round the world against prevailing winds and currents. The event takes place every four years using a one-design fleet of steel yachts, and is based on an ethos of team building using inexperienced crews. More than 200 people are selected and, while yachting experience is not necessary, they must show motivation, physical capability and mental acuity, as well as the ability to raise funds of around $40,000 to take part.

ABOVE **Chay Blyth's Global Challenge found a different formula by using a fleet of identical steel yachts.**

LEFT **The Whitbread (now Volvo) Round the World Race has developed into a gala event, as the start of the 1997 event in the Solent in the south of England shows.**

Around Alone

This race can be summarised as one person, on a sailboat, around the world, alone. It claims to be the longest race on earth for any individual in any sport, with a course spanning 43,450km (27,000 miles) including the world's roughest and most remote oceans. The race takes place every

Round the world records

1895–1898: The American, Joshua Slocum, became the pioneer of great circumnavigators when he sailed *Spray* single handed around the world.
1966: Francis Chichester (UK) 226 days solo with one stop on *Gypsy Moth IV*.
1966: Robin Lee Graham (USA) became the youngest circumnavigator of all time when he sailed *Dove* around the world at the age of 17.
1968: Robin Knox-Johnston (UK) 313 days solo non-stop in the Golden Globe Race on *Suhali*. He was the only finisher.
1971: Chay Blyth (UK) 302 days solo non-stop "wrong way round" on *British Steel*.
1973: Raymon Carlin (Mexico) 134 days fully crewed with stop-overs in Whitbread Race.
1977: Cornelius van Reischoten (Holland) 119 days fully crewed with stop-overs in Whitbread Race.

1982: Philippe Jeantot (France) 159 days solo with stop-overs in BOC (Around Alone) Challenge.
1989: Titouan Lamazou (France) 109 days solo non-stop in Vendee Globe Race.
1993: Bruno Peyron (France) 79 days non-stop in first Jules Verne Challenge.
1994: Peter Blake (New Zealand) and Robin Knox-Johnson (UK) 74 days non-stop in second Jules Verne Challenge.
1997: Olivier de Kersauson (France) 71 days non-stop in third Jules Verne Challenge.
2002: Bruno Peyron (France) skippered the 110ft catamaran *Orange* to a Jules Verne record of 64 days non-stop. Olivier de Kersauson retired with broken steering gear on his new 125ft trimaran *Geronimo*. A year later Ellen MacArthur made an attempt with the same catamaran, but lost the rig in the Southern Ocean. Kersauson failed again due to lack of wind in the Atlantic.

four years, and was originally known as the BOC Challenge when first held in 1982 – the inaugural event was won by Philippe Jeantot in 159 days.

Vendee Globe

While the Around Alone has stop-overs to allow competitors and their craft to rest and recuperate, the Vendee Globe goes one stage tougher as a single-handed marathon for monohull yachts up to 19.7m (65ft) with a non-stop, west-east course via all three capes. The race was first held in 1989 when it attracted 13 yachts, and was created by Philippe Jeantot who had already won the BOC Challenge twice running.

The America's Cup

This is probably the most sought after trophy in yachting, as well as being the most expensive to contest. Sometimes called The 'Auld' Cup, it has a history that dates back to a challenge in the mid-19th century.

1851 New York Yacht Club was invited to race in a challenge match for the Hundred Guinea Cup. Following a standing start with sails and anchors down on the start line, the schooner *America* beat a small fleet of challengers that raced once round the Isle of Wight off the south coast of England.

1857 The Hundred Guinea Cup was delivered to the New York Yacht Club,

with a deed of gift designating it as a perpetual challenge cup. It was renamed the America's Cup.

1870 The British yacht *Cambria* crossed the Atlantic to attempt to win back the cup, racing around a course off Newport, Rhode Island.

1871 *Cambria* became the first of many challengers to fail, when she suffered a 4–1 defeat by the American defender in a five race series. The "first yacht to win four races" formula has continued ever since.

1876 The American yacht *Madeline* defended a challenge by the Royal Canadian YC. This was the last America's Cup event raced in schooners.

1881–1886 The deed of gift was rewritten to specify that only one challenger and one defender should race for the cup. The American yacht *Mischief* won the right to defend, and saw off the next Canadian challenge. *Puritan* defeated *Genesta*, sent over by England's Royal Yacht Squadron. *Volunteer* defeated *Thistle*, which challenged on behalf of Scotland's Royal Clyde Yacht Club.

1893 With racing contested by J-Class yachts, the American *Vigilent* beat Britain's *Valkyrie II*. Successful American defences followed in 1895, 1899, 1901, 1903, 1920, 1930, 1934 and 1937.

1958 The first year in which the America's Cup was raced to the new 12 Metre rule, with keelboats of around 18m (60ft). *Columbia* (USA) beat *Sceptre* (UK),

with successful defences following in 1962, 1964, 1967, 1970, 1974, 1977 and 1980 against British and Australian 12 Metre yachts.

1983–1987 The Australian 12 Metre *Australia II* became the first challenger to win the America's Cup when she beat the defender *Liberty* 4–3. This ended the 132-year residency of the America's Cup at the New York Yacht Club, and the longest winning streak recorded in any sport. The American yacht *Stars & Stripes* beat Australia's defender *Kookaburra III*. The Americans took the cup back to a new home at the San Diego Yacht Club.

1992–1999 With the introduction of a new International America's Cup Class (IACC) rule for yachts of around 100ft, the Italians made an unsuccessful challenge. In 1995 the New Zealand yacht *Black Magic* helmed by Russell Coutts scored a 4–1 victory over *Young America*. The America's Cup moved to the Royal New Zealand Yacht Squadron in Auckland.

2000–2003 After one successful defence, the Royal New Zealand Yacht Squadron lost the America's Cup to the Swiss challenger *Alinghi*, which had Russell Coutts as skipper backed by a New Zealand core team.

Index

Useful addresses and acknowledgements

SAILING AUTHORITIES

Australian Yachting Federation
Locked Bag 806, Milsons Point,
NSW 2061, AUSTRALIA
tel: 02 99224333
ausyacht@ausport.gov.au
www.aussailing.org

Österreichischer Segel-Verband
Zetschegasse 21,
A-1230 Vienna, AUSTRIA
tel: 01 662 44 62-0
oesv@sailing.or.at
www.sailing.or.at

Fédération Royale Belge du Yachting
Halve Maanstraat 2C, 8620
Nieuwpoort, BELGIUM
tel: 058 23028

Canadian Yachting Association
1600 James Naismith Drive,
Gloucester
Ontario KIB 5N4, CANADA
tel: 613 7485687
sailcanada@sailing.ca
www.sailing.ca

Danish Sailing Association
Idraettens Hus, DK 2605
Broendby, DENMARK
tel: 043 262189
dan.ibsen@sejlsport.dk
www.sailing.dk

Finnish Yachting Association
Radiokatu 20, Helsinki,
FIN-00093 SLU, FINLAND
tel: 058 9 348121
aarne.kusi@splfsf.slu.fi

Fédération Française de Voile
55 Avenue Kleber, 75784 Paris
Cedex 16, FRANCE
tel: 0144058112
barbierm@compuserve.com
www.ffv.fr

Deutscher Segler-Verband
Grundgenstrasse 18, 22309
Hamburg, GERMANY
tel: 040 6320090
100763.105@compuserve.com

Hellenic Yachting Federation
51 Poseidonos Avenue, 18344
Moshato, GREECE
tel: 01 9404825
webmaster-eio@eio.gr
www.eio.gr

Irish Sailing Association
3 Park Road, Dun Laoghaire,
Co.Dublin, IRELAND
tel: 01 2800239
isa@iol.ie
www.sailing.org/isa

Federazione Italiana Vela
Corte Lambruschini, Paizza Borgo
Pila 40, Torre A - 16 piano,
16129 Genova, ITALY
tel: 010 5445 41
federvela@federvela.it
www.federvela.it

Malta Sailing Federation
PO Box 65,
Valletta, MALTA
tel: 056 337777

Yacht Club de Monaco
16 Quai Antoine 1er
MC 98000, MONACO
tel: 077 93 106300
ycm@yacht-club-monaco-mc
www.yacht-club-monaco-mc

Koninklijk Nederlands Watersport
Verbond
Postbus 87, 3980 CB Bunnik
THE NETHERLANDS
tel: 030 6566550
info@knwv.nl
www.knwv.nl

Yachting New Zealand
PO Box 33 789, Takapuna,
North Shore City
Auckland, NEW ZEALAND
tel: 09 488 9325
mail@yachtingnz.org.nz
www.yachtingnz.org.nz

Norwegian Sailing Federation
Serviceboks 1, Ullevaal Stadion,
0840 Oslo, NORWAY
tel: 021 029711
seiling@nif.idrett.no
www.nif.idrett.no/seiling

Polski Zwiazek Zeglarski
Chocimska 14,
00791 Warsaw, POLAND
tel: 022 495731
pya@polbox.com.pl
www.sailing.org.pl

Federacao Portuguesa de Vela
Doca de Belem,
1300 Lisboa, PORTUGAL
tel: 021 3647324
fpvela@fpvela.pt
www.fpvela.pt

All Russia Yachting Federation
Luchnetskaya nad.8, 119270
Moscow, RUSSIA
tel: 095 725 4703
ilyin@yachting.ru

South African Sailing
5 Vesperdene Road, Green Point,
8051 Cape Town
SOUTH AFRICA
tel: 021 4391147

sailsa@iafrica.com
www.sailing.org/rsa

Real Federacion Espanola de Vela
Luis de Salazar, 12,
28002 Madrid, SPAIN
tel: 091 5195008
info@rfev.es
www.rfev.es

Swedish Sailing Federation
Af Pontins väg 6
S-115 21 Stockholm,
SWEDEN
tel: 08 4590990
ssf@ssf.se
www.ssf.se

Swiss Sailing Federation
Haus des Sportes, Laubeggstrass
70 3000 Bern 32,
SWITZERLAND
tel: 031 359 7266
swiss_sailing@compuserve.com
www.swiss_sailing.ch

Royal Yachting Association
RYA House, Romsey Road,
Eastleigh, Hampshire SO50 9YA
UNITED KINGDOM
tel: 023 8062 7400
racing@rya.org.uk
www.rya.org.uk

US Sailing
PO Box 1260, 15 Maritime Drive,
Portsmouth, RI 02871-6015
USA
tel: 401 6830800
ussailing@compuserve.com
www.ussailing.org

ACKNOWLEDGEMENTS

The author would like to thank the following for their help, which has often been extensive:
Firstly Frazer Clark, Gael Pawson and Peter Spence of Yachts & Yachting, followed in no particular order by the RYA, ISAF, Rockley Watersports and Sail France, Minorca Sailing Holidays, Sunsail at Port Solent and in Turkey, Crewsaver, Musto, Brian Phipps of Windsport, Robin Smith, Roger Tushingham, Rob and Reg White, Rodney Pattisson, Lewmar, the Laser Centre, RS Racing, UK Sails, Sobstad, Topper International, Clamcleat, Hobie Cat and John Pierce plus a host of dinghy classes that have provided invaluable information.

The publishers would like to thank everyone at Team Unlimited in Spain. This book would not have been possible without their help. Thanks also to the models Rob Andrews, Sonia Kirk, Ioan R. Leavey, Andrew Moore, Mark Reynolds, Ewan McNeill, Felix Thornton-Jones and Ben Donald. Lastly, special thanks to Richard Langdon and Marie Rondoz of Ocean Images for the specially commissioned photography, and extensive use of their picture library.

PHOTOGRAPHY

All photography by Richard Langdon unless otherwise stated.
© Agence D.P.P.I.: page 93.
© Champion Photos: page 39tr.
© Christel clear: pages 33br, 38tl, 38tr, 38bl, 41c, 60t, 79tr, 81b, 82l, 83bl, 83br, 85lt, 85ltc, 85lc, 85lbc, 85rt, 85rc, 87lc, 87rt, 87rb & 89tl.
© Janet Harber: pages 33t, 33bl, 66t, 67t, 87lb & 88l.
© Johnathan Smith: pages 32t & 62t.
© Mark Greenberg: page 34bl.
© Mike O'Brien: page 89tr.
© Ocean Images/Richard Langdon: pages 1, 3, 6, 7b, 13, 17tr, 17b, 21b, 23b, 24t, 25tr, 27b, 28, 29, 30, 32b, 34t, 35br, 36, 37r, 38br, 39tl, 39bl, 40, 43b, 44t, 47br, 49b, 51, 69bl, 72r, 73tl, 74t, 74bl, 75, 76, 78t, 78br, 79bl, 80, 83t, 87, 87lt, 87r, 89c, 89b, 90, 91 & 92.
© Pat Collinge/Sunsail: pages 5t, 8, 34br, 37l, 52, 59t, 61t, 68, 70t, 73br, 78bl & 82r.
© Written Products/Jeremy Evans: pages 2, 7t, 10t, 11b, 12b, 14, 15, 16, 17tl, 18, 19, 20, 21t, 23t, 24b, 25b, 26, 27t, 35tl, 35tr, 35bl, 42b, 43tl, 60b, 63tl, 63c, 69t & 69br.